GENERAL COLLECTIONS

S0-ANP-645

Franklin D. Roosevelt and the Third American Revolution

Franklin D. Roosevelt and the Third American Revolution

Mario R. DiNunzio

 PRAEGER

AN IMPRINT OF ABC-CLIO, LLC
Santa Barbara, California • Denver, Colorado • Oxford, England

R0086459059

Copyright 2011 by Mario R. DiNunzio

All rights reserved. No part of this publication may be reproduced, stored in a retrieval system, or transmitted, in any form or by any means, electronic, mechanical, photocopying, recording, or otherwise, except for the inclusion of brief quotations in a review, without prior permission in writing from the publisher.

Library of Congress Cataloging-in-Publication Data

Di Nunzio, Mario R., 1936–
    Franklin D. Roosevelt and the third American revolution / Mario R. DiNunzio.
        p. cm.
    ISBN 978-0-313-39283-2 (hardcopy: alk. paper)—ISBN 978-0-313-39284-9 (ebook) 1. Roosevelt, Franklin D. (Franklin Delano), 1882–1945. 2. United States—Politics and government—1933–1945. 3. United States—Economic conditions—1918–1945. 4. New Deal, 1933–1939. I. Title.
    E806.D54   2011
    973.917092—dc22   2010051014

ISBN: 978-0-313-39283-2
EISBN: 978-0-313-39284-9

15 14 13 12 11   1 2 3 4 5

This book is also available on the World Wide Web as an eBook. Visit www.abc-clio.com for details.

Praeger
An Imprint of ABC-CLIO, LLC

ABC-CLIO, LLC
130 Cremona Drive, P.O. Box 1911
Santa Barbara, California 93116-1911

This book is printed on acid-free paper ∞

Manufactured in the United States of America

Better the occasional faults of a government that lives in a spirit of charity than the consistent omissions of a government frozen in the ice of its own indifference.

FDR—Accepting Re-nomination, June 27, 1936

The test of our progress is not whether we add more to the abundance of those who have much; it is whether we provide enough for those who have too little.

FDR—Second Inaugural, January 20, 1937

Contents

Preface

The course of the American democratic experiment was set in the colonial era even before the establishment of the United States. By 1776, each of the thirteen colonies had established governments more broadly democratic than any that people enjoyed elsewhere. Three great turning points reset the course of the experiment. The original revolution under the leadership of George Washington established democratic liberty in a national context. The second pivot came under Abraham Lincoln, whose work confirmed and extended the constitutional commitment to democratic equality as an ideal, though not well or consistently honored for decades thereafter. This book brings into focus a third revolutionary moment in American history when Franklin D. Roosevelt led the nation to recognize that the democratic experiment and the promise of the founding fathers required a broad commitment to fraternity, that common effort to secure and expand the general welfare of citizens. It was an idea both implied and explicit in the founding documents of the republic.

Roosevelt saw that the requirements of a healthy democracy and the demands of simple justice called for a greater measure of material security. His New Deal adapted the democratic agenda accordingly. That adjustment required new and much expanded action by government to secure the blessings of liberty and equality by establishing mechanisms for more effective fraternal support and security.

Americans have argued about the proper role of a national government ever since the struggle over the ratification of the Constitution and the conflicting appeals of Alexander Hamilton and Thomas Jefferson in the Washington administration. That America, at the end of the 18th century, was a small, rural, and agrarian society. Franklin Roosevelt led a large, increasingly urban, and heavily industrial society in the fourth decade of the 20th century. The fundamental goals of the American democracy remained the same, but he saw that a new age and new circumstances dictated a new role for the national government. Roosevelt changed the economic reality of class in the United States, and for this, some could not forgive him. Resistance to the changes he wrought was narrow but intense, and the support of the American people for his New Deal was overwhelming. The national debate over the powers and responsibilities of the national government thus begun continues to our own day. The Roosevelt revolution changed the United States. Those who have inherited and admire his vision believe that more needs to be done. Perhaps the story of the Roosevelt revolution can offer some insight into the role of government demanded by a 21st century society.

In these pages we examine the Roosevelt revolution in its historical context and through the words of Franklin D. Roosevelt himself. The speeches and fireside chats collected here contain the elements of Roosevelt's political and presidential philosophy. Embedded here are the roots of his thinking that arose from his personal, political, and religious experience. His ideas moved from emergency responses to the crisis of the Great Depression upon his taking office to the establishment of permanent structures to provide for the security and welfare of the American people. His words have been edited for context and appropriate length while retaining the substance of his thought. The use of *** indicates material deleted. While he employed speechwriters, especially Samuel I. Rosenman, FDR was very active in shaping his speeches in style and substance. The clear trajectory and consistency of thought presented here stand as evidence of the moral and intellectual foundation of the Roosevelt revolution.

Introduction

As the ship crept smoothly past the welcoming Statue of Liberty in New York harbor, a young man named Joseph felt a strange mix of fear and hope about the future. Apprenticed to a barber at twelve, the future promised little in his village, and so now in his twenties, he came to America for a new start. A good beginning was ambushed by the terror of the Great Depression, but with time, long hours of labor, and a good wife, life showed promise. They were able finally to buy a modest house, raise three sons, and see them through university education, professional careers, and prosperity. This story is astonishing not because it is unique, but because it is so ordinary. With adjustments to accommodate individual differences of heritage and history, it is a story that could be repeated in its essentials by millions of American families. This story and the uncounted others like it were written by the Roosevelt revolution.

Franklin D. Roosevelt's New Deal transformed a proletariat into a new class and in doing so fulfilled one of the promises of the original American Revolution. In the process Roosevelt saved American capitalism from its own excesses and won the enduring hatred of those thus rescued. Their venom was stirred not only by the cost of economic reform (any suggestion of even modest levels of taxation implied the demonic), but also and perhaps more intensely because this new revolution threatened the privileged status in American society that reserved to them a self-defined superiority. The first American Revolution did not embrace a leveling radicalism, but it did hold the promise of civic equality and social mobility in a free society. That promise, subsequent history, and the New Deal required an uncomfortable adjustment of thought among American elites.

The founding document of the United States of America is the Declaration of Independence, which, in addition to justifying separation from Great Britain, also established a theoretical basis for the obligations of government. The appointed duty of government was to protect and defend the Creator-given, natural rights that belonged to a free, equal, and fraternal people. The first American Revolution, Washington's revolution, proclaimed American freedom—that ideal of *liberty*, an act of faith that a broad community of ordinary people could govern themselves—and succeeding generations struggled to realize more fully that ideal. Property qualifications for political participation gradually melted away, and by the age of Jackson in the 1830s universal suffrage became the norm for men and the goal for all. Lincoln's revolution enshrined in the law and in an amended Constitution Jefferson's majestic proclamation of human *equality*. And perfecting the just realization of that ideal was the work of more than a century and continues still. Franklin Roosevelt's New Deal looked to the fulfillment of the third revolutionary ideal–*fraternity*, the idea that a community of free and equal people is obliged to offer the fundamentals of human well-being to all its members as a matter of right. The concept was as revolutionary as the affirmed ideals of liberty and equality.

The logic of this obligation to fraternity is embedded in Jefferson's Declaration. There is a fraternal bond among the children of the Creator and a duty among people who unite as one nation and establish a government whose fundamental purpose is "to protect these rights." The age of the Enlightenment was deeply secular and sought some distance from organized religious structure, but the ethics of Enlightenment thinkers were impressively Judeo-Christian ethics in secular dress. Immanuel Kant's categorical imperative sought a kind of universal golden rule by philosophical rather than religious dictation. That human beings are free and equal in the eyes of the Creator was celebrated but not invented by Enlightenment thinkers like Jefferson. A free will and equality before God resided deeply in Western religious tradition. So, too, Enlightenment thought cast the very traditional obligation of fraternal caring into its revolutionary diction. When the American founders crafted a preamble for the new Constitution in 1787, they acknowledged a basic goal of this more perfect union was "to promote the general welfare." Liberty implies equality, and equality implies fraternity.

It was this third revolutionary ideal that animated the Roosevelt revolution. Long embedded in the democratic experiment, the obligation of government to underwrite a measure of security and well-being for Americans became more explicit in the New Deal. The industrial revolution, the transformation of capitalism in the 19th century, and the urbanization of society recast the role of government and community in relation to the general welfare that the Constitution pledged to promote. Roosevelt understood those changes, and he understood that meaningful liberty and equality required a measure of material well-being. The work began in earnest with the New Deal, continued in the decades that followed, and slowed some during regimes uncongenial to the thought. As the ideals of liberty and equality have required time and struggle to be more fully realized, so too, the fraternal ideal championed by Roosevelt demands yet more of this young century. Roosevelt's revolution remains incomplete when, in this prosperous and powerful nation, pockets of poverty, an inadequate health care system by the standards of the developed world, and flaccid government oversight in the face of dangerous economic gymnastics persist.

1

The First Revolution

The American Revolution that began in 1776 was a war for independence from Great Britain and a radical effort to achieve a measure of liberty, equality, and fraternity for Americans. Years later those words made up the iconic slogan of the French Revolution, but that rising was betrayed by its makers and degenerated into vengeance and self-destructive violence. France and all of Europe had little experience with democratic practice. Rousseau struggled with the concept in *The Social Contract* but conceded that genuine democracy would work if men were angels, but not in this mortal world. He designed, instead, the model for a small republic in which public debate of political issues would be banned, a kind of deism would stand as the official state religion, and men would be, in his words, forced to be free. Statues of Rousseau were raised during the radical days of the French Revolution, but the movement toward democracy faltered. When Robespierre and the Jacobins took control of the revolution a pattern was established for future revolutions that promised democracy but delivered tyranny. In France, as later in Russia, China, Cuba, and elsewhere, democracy was on its way, but it had to await the elimination of foreign dangers and enemies of the revolution. The enemies were legion and, alas, the wait was long and empty. Parisian streets lay blood stained, and in the end a Napoleonic dictatorship smothered the revolution.

It was the American Revolution that endured and struggled to fulfill the hopes implied in the slogan. The American experience was unique in the world of the late 18th century in producing a democratic polity that went beyond the expectations and even the desires of some of the founders. Its immediate success was winning liberty and independence from British control, but much more than independence was at stake in the American struggle.

The hapless British leadership of the day did not understand their American colonies and decided the task at hand was simply to quell the uprising of unruly colonial ruffians. They could not appreciate the degree of freedom and the local institutions of self-government that all of the American colonies enjoyed, some for over a century. From the planting of Jamestown and the Pilgrims' landing at Plymouth, Americans had had to fend for themselves. On their own, they had to hack a living out of the woods and organize communities at a great distance from governing authority. Historian Frederick Jackson Turner, in a famous address to the American Historical Association in 1893, insisted that the roots of American democracy lay not in Europe, but in this frontier experience that ran continuously from the earliest settlements to the westward movement through one generation after another.[1] Crucially important in this process was the essentially egalitarian nature of the experience, especially in the middle and northern colonies. Up to and beyond the revolution, there were few of the great disparities of wealth and status that marked so sharply the classes of European society. The frontier experience in America produced a paradoxical combination of rugged individualism and communal cooperation. Survival in the primitive conditions of colonial life demanded hard work, vigor, sobriety, and determined personal and familial effort. It also powerfully encouraged neighbors to join together for barn raising, land clearing, and path breaking—those heavy projects too burdensome for one man or one family alone.

Perhaps even more important than frontier conditions, for these moderated with time, was the great distance from governing powers. Colonial Americans were an ocean away from careful oversight by crown and parliament, and they were days and weeks and hard terrain away from colonial authorities as they became established. In governance, as in the requirements of daily life, they had to do for themselves. So in establishing local rules and local governments in such a society, who was to be excluded? From the beginning, this was a society of broad landownership, in most cases involving holdings of modest dimensions. It was a society in which one's lineage, one's fine linens, and one's smart clothes mattered little to survival or status. The lives of most colonials were most directly touched by local governments, and local governments tended toward democratic practice. They were too distant for careful oversight by the British, and the developing democratic practice of these societies escaped the attention, or at least the concern, of an imperial government focused more on economic matters and, in any case, more interested in its more lucrative West Indian possessions. For over a century before the 1760s, neglect of the continental colonies was more normal than close supervision and direction. Regulations imposed by London were relatively few, mildly burdensome, and when inconvenient, evaded with scant fear of discovery or penalty. On their own, the American colonists were free to shape their world anew.

Colonial Americans created the most egalitarian society in the Western world not out of the blueprint of a radical ideology, but out of the material and social circumstances into which they settled. Under these conditions of rough equality and great diversity in religion and ethnicity (particularly in the middle colonies), ideas about limiting participation in governance died quickly. Early attempts at religious tests even in Puritan New England, for example, did not survive the second generation. Property qualifications persisted longer, but property, as noted, was widely held and produced broad electorates. While a colonial elite with pretensions to aristocracy existed, it "was never as well established, never as wealthy, never as dominant as it would have liked."[2] A measure of democracy unknown anywhere in the world existed in America *before* 1776.

When Great Britain defeated France in the Seven Years' War (the French and Indian War in America), the Treaty of Paris in 1763 enlarged the empire with ceded French possessions. The victory and the spoils, however, came at great expense. The British government was determined to reorganize the enlarged empire for greater control and efficiency. Part of the plan was to have the Americans, liberated by British arms from the harassing efforts of the French and their Indian allies, help pay down a share of the enormous debt accrued by this effort. Thus the parade of new taxes and rules beginning in 1763: the proclamation confining colonists east of the Appalachians, the Sugar Act of 1664, the Stamp Act of 1665, the Townshend Act of 1667, and more. The aim and the demands were not entirely unreasonable, but the execution was clumsy, insensitive, and offensive to American colonists. An inept British government converted a group of colonies so jealous of each other that they rejected Benjamin Franklin's 1854 Albany Plan for a joint effort against French frontier assaults into a united force capable of revolution. What began as protests by loyal subjects of the king against new regulations and taxes, officious errors, and indifferent stubbornness was transformed into what Americans saw as a struggle for self-government and freedom. London did not understand the problem was not that the control they were trying to impose on the Americans was so unjust; it was simply too late. The American Revolution was a fight for independence in order to preserve local democracies and establish a people of liberty as a national entity.

Jefferson's Declaration of Independence articulates the American mind of 1776 producing an eloquent expression of democratic faith. He posits an egalitarianism without exception. Surely a writer of Jefferson's skill, in committee with men like John Adams and Benjamin Franklin, could have finessed the language to account for the reality of a persistent slavery. But this document spoke to the ages. "*All* men are created equal." Like Jefferson, Lincoln knew that liberty and justice demanded equality. Adding to the radicalism of the Declaration is the logic that equality demands fraternity. "In the context of the Declaration, the concept of the state is superfluous. Sovereignty resides in the people who establish government to serve them. No overriding state is necessary to embody the nation, to demand obedience, to create romantic fictions of destiny and grandeur. In the Declaration there is no *patria*. Paternity is in the Creator, not the fatherland. It is not patriotism that is commanded. The real foundation of loyalty and service is among brothers [children of the Creator] to each other. It is fraternity."[3]

Such was the revolution George Washington led, and it was his heroic action and political wisdom that made its success possible. He assembled and held together a ragtag army under extreme conditions, through repeated setbacks and retreats, and with the most limited resources. He devised the hit-and-run tactics appropriate to the American landscape and his army's limited resources, eventually exhausting British patience, and outmaneuvering the vastly superior forces of the Empire. His was the work of strategic genius and inspired leadership. After the victory, Washington's desire to retire to his Mount Vernon estate was repeatedly frustrated by renewed calls to public service. He encouraged reshaping the infant nation's constitutional structure, and his commanding presence at the Convention of 1787 sustained the delegates through a hot summer of factional divisions and divergent sectional and state interests.

Had Americans gone too far toward democracy under the Articles of Confederation? Was the call for constitutional revision a conservative movement of nervous elites? Or was the United States under the Articles too constrained by localized state interests to survive as a healthy nation worthy of recognition by a watching world? These questions have long engaged historians. The leaders of the revolutionary generation, Washington foremost among them, conceded to the need for a more visible and stable structure of union. In the reigning circumstances of political unrest, economic hard times, and dubious national credit in the eyes of the world, Americans ratified the decision of their leaders. The new Constitution became ". . . as Madison pointed out, a charter of power granted by liberty rather than, as in Europe, a charter of liberty granted by power."[4]

Washington was again called, now to serve as president under the new Constitution, and again he set aside his private interests. With stoic patience he used all his political judgment and mediating skill to sustain the democratic experiment through the factionalism of an emergent political party system not clearly provided for in the Constitution. In both domestic and foreign affairs, Thomas Jefferson and Alexander Hamilton vied for Washington's assent to conflicting policies and philosophies of government. Future generations of Americans took for granted the success of this experiment in liberty which was, in fact, by no means certain. Washington provided the good judgment and firm hand that kept the fragile ship of state sailing and the hope alive in the earliest days of the adventure.

As the revolutionary dust settled, the new nation stood alone in the world as a living democracy, and European elites were uncertain whether to laugh or cry. Leaders of the European Enlightenment sought rational government, but democrats were rare among them. The idea that peasants (they called them farmers in America) should vote and hold office was laughable in enlightened European political thought. Collapse of the foolish experiment in America they deemed inevitable and welcome. But it did not collapse, and thus the tears. The American nation survived and thrived in the new order of political ideas. The Washington revolution was not fully complete in his lifetime, but democratic liberties did expand. By the presidency of Andrew Jackson property qualifications for voting disappeared almost everywhere (Rhode Island and South Carolina providing errant exception), and something close to universal suffrage (albeit white and male) was the rule.

That process of expanding and perfecting American liberty continued through the decades into the 20th century toward a genuine universal suffrage. But from the days of the original Washington revolution, even if incomplete, the American democratic experiment stood alone as the beacon to the world. Reform and revolutionary movements across Europe throughout the 19th century looked not to French failure but to American success. The Chartists in England pointed to the United States as the model for British reform. The aim of Giuseppe Mazzini's Young Italy Movement was the establishment of an American style democratic republic. Many travelers, Alexis de Tocqueville foremost among them, described the American experiment warts and all. The impact was powerful. From Scandinavia to Italy and from Great Britain to Russia, American democratic liberty inspired calls for reform or revolt. "If Americans can enjoy prosperity *and* liberty, why can't we?" Throughout the 19th century millions answered the question; they came to America. Apologies to Marx, it was the specter of democracy that haunted Europe.

2

The Second Revolution

The American Revolution of George Washington introduced a democratic republic to a world dominated by monarchy and aristocracy. Civic equality lay at the heart of republicanism, and in America republicanism was democratic, and democracy fostered the egalitarian spirit of a new society. This, perhaps, made inevitable a second revolution to perfect the first. From the start Americans had reason to be both proud and embarrassed. They could be proud because the world looked to the United States, some fearful of its example, others inspired by its success and its promise. Embarrassment lay in the stark fact that the most democratic polity in the world persisted longer than most in sustaining the institution of human slavery.

Many of the revolutionaries, including Washington and Jefferson, were slave owners and troubled by the persistence of the institution. Jefferson, so skilled with language, did not qualify his declaration that all men were created equal. The question for many during the earliest days of the republic was not *whether* to get rid of slavery, but *how* to do it. For the sake of revolutionary unity and in the face of resistance to ideas of emancipation from southern states like South Carolina and Georgia, the issue was compromised into the background. Northern states arranged for emancipation, and the external slave trade was scheduled for extinction, but slavery endured. After the turn of the 19th century and the surge of a cotton culture suited to gang labor, the southern commitment to slavery hardened. Apologists now defended the institution as part of the southern "way of life" and culture, disguising the powerful commercial imperative to maintain a system of slave labor. Before 1820 most anti-slave societies were located and did their work in the South; by 1830 they had disappeared there, and anti-slavery advocacy in the South was dangerous to health and life itself.

Decades of drifting apart on the issue of slavery intensified political tensions between North and South. The Missouri Compromise of 1820 deflected a crisis, but a perceptive Jefferson read the dispute as "a fire bell in the night." The admission of Missouri, with slaves, would have upset the balance of free and slave states. The compromise provided for the separation of Maine from Massachusetts, clearing the path for the admission of Maine as a free state and Missouri as a slave state. For the moment, the issue was settled, but the impending crisis was only postponed, not eliminated.

Continuing tension gave way to anger after 1848, when victory over Mexico added potential slave territory to the United States. By then respected southern writers like George Fitzhugh and political leaders like John Calhoun had convinced many in the South that slavery must expand or die. They saw a more rapidly growing northern popula-tion and recognized the danger that the South could be overwhelmed should an array of territories be admitted to the Union as free states. Southerners began to demand that settlers be allowed to bring slaves into the western territories in the hope that new slave states would result. Another compromise in 1850, allowing California into the union as a free state, again only delayed the showdown.

The issue exploded in 1854 with the passage of the Kansas-Nebraska Act. Its principal sponsor was Senator Stephen Douglas, Democrat of Illinois, who sought a solution through the idea of "popular sover-eignty." He proposed to let the people of a territory decide for them-selves whether to enter the union as a free or slave state. The idea appealed to many Southerners and some in the North. But even as the South settled more firmly into the position that slavery must expand, majority opinion in the North now insisted there should be no further extension of slave territory in the United States.

The issue was powerful enough to throw the American political system into confusion and to recast the party system. Over the next two years, the Whig Party collapsed, the Democrats split into factions, new parties dedicated to halting the spread of slavery were born, and nativist parties grew in response to the massive immigration of recent years. After months of political jockeying, party apostasy, and fusion movements, a new Republican Party confronted the damaged and divided Democrats. The Republicans included former Whigs—those Democrats who opposed the popular sovereignty idea, Free-Soilers, abolitionists, and nativist Know-Nothings. These groups had little in common. Some had a history as old enemies dating back to the battles between Jacksonian Democrats and Whigs. Some were high-tariff men; some favored lower tariffs. Some were hostile to immigrants and Catholics; some were Catholic immigrants. Abolitionists favored immediate emancipation, but many Republicans thought the abolitionists dangerously radical. The one issue that held this unwieldy coalition together was their uncompromising opposition to the spread of slavery into new territories.

Meanwhile the South grew more determined than ever to protect its "way of life," and talk of secession moved from the fringes closer to the center of southern politics. Tempers flared ominously. One day in May 1857, Preston Brooks, congressman from South Carolina, approached the desk of anti-slavery Senator Charles Sumner of Massachusetts, raised his cane high and beat Sumner into unconsciousness to redress a perceived insult in a recent speech by the senator. Southern newspaper editorials applauded Brooks, and sectional tensions grew still more bitter. Also in 1857, the Supreme Court rendered its Dred Scott decision, which entitled Southerners to bring their slave "property" with them into the territories. Abraham Lincoln's most telling challenge to Stephen Douglas in their famous senate campaign debates in 1858 came when he asked Douglas how his popular sovereignty solutions could work in the face of the Court's decision. Could a majority of the people of any prospective state successfully keep slavery out? Douglas, clearly a figure of presidential stature and ambition, fumbled and responded weakly. During the next two years, sectional tension grew worse. Such was the setting of American politics during the 1850s, when relations between the North and the South moved steadily from strident politics toward disunion and war.

When Abraham Lincoln came within a whisker of unseating Senator Douglas, leader of the Democrats and the best known political figure in the country in 1858, he became something of a hero to Republicans. A successful speaking tour across the North and skillful maneuvers at the national party convention in 1860 rocketed him ahead of the favorites to a nomination for president. During the campaign, as he had in the past, Lincoln sustained the key Republican position on slavery. He insisted that a Republican victory posed no threat to slavery in the South, but the opposition to the *expansion* of slavery was absolute. Within days of his election, the secession of Southern states began with South Carolina, for decades the vanguard of Southern radicalism, leading the way. Frantic efforts at compromise marked the interregnum right up to Inauguration Day. Lincoln was flexible on several points concerning slavery, including the enforcement of fugitive slave laws, and he was willing to reassure the South that neither he nor his party would assault slavery in the states where it existed. For Southerners this was not enough; they insisted that their ability to transport slaves into the territories be recognized as a constitutional right of property. But Lincoln would not compromise on the issue of expansion; that had brought his party into being and that was the only issue that held it together. And the war came.

Lincoln's immediate objective as president was the preservation of the union, which he called "the world's best hope." He thought it so because, in a world not yet receptive to broad participatory democracy, it was the success of the American experiment that inspired the democratic reform movements across Europe. Lincoln knew well that the collapse of the union would encourage the enemies of democracy and could bury the hopes of those longing to imitate the American example. The voices of reaction would surely associate democracy with political chaos and civil war, and they would ask why good order and stability should be threatened by a system of rule by the ignorant masses. Those voices were still strong, and once the war began the ruling houses of Europe, almost unanimously, favored the South and the break-up of the union. From his first objective to preserve the union Lincoln never wavered, but he soon broadened his vision of that democratic union. It was quickly clear to him that slavery could not and ought not survive the war. And so, he took advantage of the first substantial union military victory at Antietam in September 1862, to declare emancipation a war aim. Some critics of acutely narrow vision have noted that Lincoln's order applied only to those slaves behind enemy lines, and thus at the moment of its proclamation freed no slaves and did not apply at all to slaves in the border areas under union control. The argument is inane, for it was clear to all, North and South, that the Emancipation Proclamation made an end to slavery everywhere inevitable given a union victory. Indeed the passage and ratification of the Thirteenth Amendment settled the matter. An important question left open was the civic status of emancipated African Americans.

Months before the war was over Lincoln began to lay plans to repair the political relations among the states of a restored union. What has been called "Lincoln's Plan" for reconstruction reached for quick and relatively easy return of the rebellious states to full representation in

Congress. While some in Congress would like to have levied punishing terms on the South, Lincoln's ideas of generous reconciliation had broad political support. But before Lincoln could see his rules applied across the South, assassination ended his agile and wise leadership in the second week of April 1865, even as the country celebrated the end of the war. Events in the South in the months that followed gave many who had supported Lincoln's plan second thoughts about easy restoration, and by the end of the year Congress set a new course.

Across the South, white leaders still in control of state and local governments enacted the Black Codes, sets of laws severely restricting the freedom of those recently liberated. Limits on travel, restrictions on assembly, and especially draconian vagrancy laws carrying forced labor penalties were seen as poorly veiled attempts to reinstitute a form of servitude. Had the slaughter of four years of war been suffered only to return to pre-war conditions? Eric Foner reminds us that Lincoln considered his reconstruction plans as experiments and "he would never have allowed his own position to be compromised by shortcomings of the South."[1]

When the Thirty-Ninth Congress reconvened in December, not just the radicals among the Republicans, but those who had fully supported Lincoln's benign ideas for reconstruction called for some assurance that the war had not been fought in vain. Outraged by news of the Black Codes, Congress passed two key measures. The Freedmen's Bureau Act extended the life and enlarged the powers of the agency established to assist African Americans in the transition to freedom. The Civil Rights Act, the first in American history, effectively declared that freedmen (and anyone born in the United States) were citizens and entitled to all the rights of citizens. Southerners were assured that cooperation with this legislation would clear the way to smooth and rapid reconstruction. Southern opinion was hostile, and a sympathetic President Andrew Johnson vetoed both bills. An angry Congress overrode the vetoes by huge margins and took steps to put equal rights provisions beyond the reach of any future unfriendly court or Congress. Republican majorities converted the core of the Civil Rights Act into the Fourteenth Amendment and sent it on to the states for ratification.

What unfolded was a telling moment in American history. The Fourteenth Amendment, which applied not just to the South but nationwide, was solidly approved by the Northern states and uniformly rejected by the Southern states. This was more proof for some that the

South did not intend to accept the consequences of defeat. This episode also served as introduction to a brief period of about three years during which the people of the North were fully committed to equal rights for black Americans. The Northern states would soon ratify the Fifteenth Amendment in support of black voting rights, and in the fall of 1866 Northern states elected a Congress with even larger majorities in support of black rights. In the face of presidential intransigence and obstruction (Johnson tried to block both amendments and resorted to intemperate language in attacking Congress while reportedly inebriated), Republicans moved to take control of the reconstruction process. They forced the Southern states to rewrite their constitutions to provide for black civil and voting rights and installed new governments including black officeholders across the South. "The American vision of republican liberty encompassed more than simple freedom, it included also civil and political equality of freedmen."[2]

Lincoln was always pragmatic and flexible in his politics and always open to new directions to meet changing conditions. That he would have clung rigidly to his easy plan for reconstruction in the face of Southern actions overtly hostile to genuine emancipation is extremely unlikely. Full citizenship and equal rights were the logical sequels to emancipation, and therein lay the Lincoln revolution. Properly interpreted, what was done in the years between 1865 and 1868 was all that was necessary to establish the principle of equal citizenship in a democratic society. Reconstruction was a "stunning and unprecedented experiment in interracial democracy." Of those that abolished slavery in the 19th century, the United States was the only country to confer equal citizenship to former slaves. Then the country rejected its own achievement and freed African Americans were "abandoned by the nation, [and] fell victim to violence and fraud."[3] The Northern commitment to black rights, so clear in those years, soon faded.

Over time contrived judicial interpretations set back the cause of equality, most famously with the "separate but equal" ruling of a later Supreme Court. Organizations like the Ku Klux Klan used intimidation and violence with little fear of the law, and the national press and public responded to outrage with indifference. Racial and ethnic discrimination was tolerated and encouraged even outside the South. Nevertheless, the Lincoln revolution reaffirmed Jefferson's principle of equality indelibly, and that haunted the conscience of democratic America. It also inspired, against discouraging odds, the persistent and often painful struggle to convert ideal into reality. Booker T. Washington,

W. E. B. Du Bois, A. Philip Randolph, Thurgood Marshall, Martin Luther King Jr., Rosa Parks, and a host of unsung heroes challenged the prejudice disguised as legal precision and insisted on the ideal. The long civil rights march of the 20th century climbed mountains and threaded through narrow passes to reach what King called the promised land of equality. The Lincoln revolution transformed the nation with the recognition that liberty demanded equality. The journey from Abraham Lincoln to Barack Obama was a long trek to fulfill the revolutionary ideal of equality. The realist looks not for perfection but for measurable progress, and now that progress must be clear even to the cynic. Revolutions themselves tend to be brief, but fulfilling American revolutionary ideals has been an interminable process that still continues.

3

Roots

The world of modern industrial and finance capitalism that emerged in the late 19th century presented a new challenge to the American democratic experiment and its ideals. After the Civil War, industrial capitalism migrated from what had been a highly competitive stage of what were usually owner-managed manufacturing enterprises of modest size to a monopolistic era of trust building and owner absentee big business. The result was a fabulous growth of American industry stimulated by a combination of inventive genius, congenial government policies, corruption, and the exploitation of labor. The subsidizing largesse of a generous and protective government, the innovative constitution bending of a sympathetic Supreme Court, and the ingenious organizing skill of men like J. P. Morgan and John D. Rockefeller transformed American capitalism.

Advocates of unfettered free enterprise were dogmatically committed to resisting the "fetters" of even the most modest levels of regulation. But they were quite agile in preaching that doctrine while accepting all possible government assistance. The federal government continued to impose high tariffs on imports, no longer necessary to protect infant industries struggling against crippling foreign imports. High tariffs levied during the Civil War to help finance the struggle continued undiminished for decades even on products that could have easily undersold foreign competitors and still turned a generous profit. Great fortunes were made, both honestly and by imaginative theft, from government subsidies for railroad building. Land grants to railroads by states and the federal government eventually totaled acreage equal to the dimensions of Texas. This was automatically valuable land; it bordered rail lines! Oakes Ames, congressman from Massachusetts, and the Credit Mobilier Corporation drained the Union Pacific Railroad of its capital from both the huge government subsidies and from private investors. Gross over-billing for shoddy work and phantom construction drove the Union Pacific into bankruptcy while it enriched the favored investors of Credit Mobilier.

In a series of cases after the Civil War, a business-friendly Supreme Court added imaginatively to the original intent of the Fourteenth Amendment in developing a doctrine of "substantive due process" aimed at protecting the property rights of corporations. Recognizing corporations as "persons" under the law, the Court read the language of the amendment that no person shall be deprived of "life, liberty, or property without due process of law" as a defense against government regulation of corporations. For decades the Court stood guard against efforts at economic regulation or reform and invested laissez-faire capitalism with extraordinary power and license.

Through shared inclinations obviating the need for conspiracy, the courts and the capitalists, while enlarging the rights of corporations, combined to subvert any modest sign of organized power among the working class. The law was interpreted to hamper unionization, weaken bargaining power, limit the use of strikes, and sustain low wages. When the law faltered, strong-arm tactics, blackballing, scabs, strike breakers, and violence enforced the corporate will.

Oil literally and financially lubricated the American industrial machine. The exploitation of petroleum spawned new industries and transformed old ones. John D. Rockefeller entered the business of oil refining in the 1870s, impressed by the potential of the industry but dismayed by the high degree of competition among dozens of refineries. His lawyers experimented with various organizing devices until they hit on a form of trust organization, the holding company, which survived legal challenges from the states. A holding company is a corporation that controls other corporations by owning a controlling portion of their stock. This could be a small percentage of stock as long as it was more than any other investor could assemble. The plan worked wonders. Rockefeller soon controlled more than 90 percent of the oil refining in the United States. His Standard Oil Company, progenitor of the modern Esso and Exxon, expanded its power to control or profoundly influence oil wells, transport facilities, distributorships, and eventually even retail outlets. The Rockefeller fortune became legendary, and by the end of the century the oil industry was only one Rockefeller interest. The money opened the way into finance capitalism through banking and the control of varied industries.

The Rockefeller model was imitated as one industry after another was monopolized by trust building. Among the most successful at the game was Andrew Carnegie in the steel industry. What Rockefeller did to oil, Carnegie did to steel. For the year 1900 Carnegie's personal income topped $30 million, unencumbered by corporate or income taxes. Satisfied with his achievement and wanting to do some good with his money, Carnegie decided to retire from the steel business and sold his interests to J. P. Morgan. Morgan combined Carnegie Steel with a few operations that had escaped the monopoly and created the first company worth more than $1 billion, United States Steel Corporation. As impressive as Morgan's acquisition was, what was more impressive was the fact that U. S. Steel amounted to a side-line for Morgan. He was the leading finance capitalist in the United States, and his House of Morgan controlled dozens of large corporations including railroads, shipping interests, other banks, insurance companies, and manufacturing enterprises.

The great success of the monopolists and financiers who directed the explosive American economy created aggregates of fabulous wealth that translated into unchallenged power. The Morgans and Rockefellers of the age exercised a kind of power over the health and well-being of people and communities that was once the prerogative only of governments. And they used this power without the inconvenient obligation to submit their performance to the judgment of an electorate. The story is often told that when a rich colleague thinking of a similar purchase asked J. P. Morgan how much his yacht cost, he was told, "If you have to ask, you can't afford it." The tale is intended as an impressive affirmation of wealth, but Morgan's power is better illustrated by his rescue of Grover Cleveland. During the economic crash of 1894, gold fled the U. S. Treasury at such a pace that President Cleveland was informed his government would run out of money in a matter of months. The president's effort to bring gold in through the sale of government bonds sputtered weakly. He turned to Morgan for help. The House of Morgan enjoyed greater credibility than the U. S. government, so bonds backed by Morgan sold briskly. Gold flowed into the Treasury, the government remained solvent, and the crisis passed. Morgan, elected to no public office, wielded more effective economic power than the president of the United States. Morgan's patriotic service was made all the sweeter by the millions paid him in commissions for the sale of the bonds.

American liberal political thought of the day, such as existed, was dominated by a continuing Jeffersonian tradition that was suspicious of strong government. To the reigning capitalists this was a congenial doctrine. Governing power should be confined as much as possible, dogma dictated, to state and local government, within reach of the people. Those were, of course, also within easy reach and influence of the resourceful entrepreneur. Reformers railed against the corruption and the abuses of the moneyed classes, but they handcuffed themselves with Jeffersonian fears that government was itself the greatest danger to liberty. That was an idea of some relevance to the revolutionary generation of the 18th century, but by the end of the 19th century, it was rendered archaic in an age when New York bankers exercised more influence in the day-to-day workings of society than did the national government. Jefferson could not have imagined the intensity of concentrated power generated by the new industrial order. It was that power, exercised for the private interest and responsible to no electorate, that stood as a new danger to democracy. It would require decades for the liberal or progressively inclined to overcome their crippling Jeffersonian prejudice.

It was no accident, then, that the first effective confrontation with entrenched capitalist power from the mainstream of American politics came not from Progressives who admired Jefferson, but from Theodore Roosevelt, who did not. In Europe the response to modern capitalist power was embodied in a variety of Marxist prescriptions on the left, and eventually by the creation of the fascist super-state on the right. The American response to the realities of industrial capitalist power was different. The United States sought to harness the power of the new capitalism through government regulation. That work was begun by the first Roosevelt, enlarged by Woodrow Wilson, and effectively completed by Franklin Roosevelt. What passed for a progressive or liberal economic philosophy was a middle way between unfettered, individualist, free market capitalism and centralized, Marxist socialism. Little genuinely new in this regard has emerged since the New Deal. Americans have argued about too much regulation as against not enough regulation, but the essential American response has persisted.

The late-20th-century conservative passion for deregulation that began with the Reagan presidency represented a rejection of much of the New Deal formula, and, to the more fervent, the beginning of a revolution to undo other key New Deal measures like Social Security. The deregulation panacea in which both Democrats and Republicans were complicit (its promise was wealth creation virtually limitless in breadth and intensity) was heavily responsible for the financial collapse of 2008. This passion for deregulation that often expressed itself by identifying government itself as "the problem" clearly implied a rejection of Roosevelt's New Deal revolution, which had its roots in an American reform tradition that began in the previous century.

Throughout the 19th century the United States experienced periodic surges of reform activism. The Revolutionary generation itself sought to extend democratic ideas and participation. The age of Andrew Jackson saw reform movements organized to correct an array of social ills. These included the anti-slavery crusade, as well as organizations to secure women's rights, prison reform, better care of the mentally ill, labor reform, improvements in education, and they extended even to utopian communal experiments. Free-Soil and abolition were the principal reform causes of the pre-war decades in the North.

After the Civil War, the early responses to the rigors that an expansive industrial age heaped on the laboring classes came not only from radical socialist groups of various types, but from American churches as well. Radical solutions have never successfully appealed to the American electorate, but religious support for reform had a broader influence on public perceptions. A number of young Protestant ministers like Washington Gladden and Walter Rauschenbusch preached what came to be known as the Social Gospel. They decried the dangers and brutality of unregulated working conditions, supported workers in unionizing efforts, and called for government action to alleviate the worst conditions born of a callous industrial machine. Among Catholics, whose numbers were heavily immigrant and predominantly working-class in this era, bishops like Edward Cardinal Gibbons and priests like Monsignor John Ryan paralleled the work of their Protestant counterparts in spreading the Social Gospel.

Meanwhile, the last decades of the century saw the emergence of two political movements troubled by the pernicious influence of capitalism on American life. One was the agrarian Populist movement, which, in its long list of reform ideas to improve the lot of the nation's farm families, championed stronger government action to counter and control the power of capital. The Populists were representative mainly of rural and agrarian Americans, but by the 1890s out of city and state governments there emerged the Progressive movement. Early Progressive efforts focused on ending Gilded Age corruption in government at all levels, but Progressives soon broadened their vision and saw the deeper causes of that corruption lay in distorted economic and social conditions. By 1900 Populism declined, but an important remnant, of which William Jennings Bryan was the symbol, merged with the Progressives in a campaign of national reform. In the campaign of 1896, Bryan, the Democratic standard-bearer, was also nominated by the Populists to stand against the conservative Republican, William McKinley.

After 1900, a national Progressive movement with leaders like Democrat Bryan and Republican Robert Lafollette of Wisconsin pushed and prodded both parties in the direction of economic and political reform. Their ideas were supported by the revelations of the "muckrakers," journalists who exposed many of the abuses associated with the corrupting influence of unregulated capital. It was this progressivism that supplied the ideas and energy for an era of change that came with the presidencies of Theodore Roosevelt and Woodrow Wilson.

Theodore Roosevelt was the first president to raise the alarm about the power of unbridled capital. A young and professedly conservative Theodore Roosevelt ridiculed progressive reformers as "do-gooders." But political experience and the responsibilities of the presidency worked changes in his thought. In his political career, Roosevelt had always been a "regular" in a broadly conservative party, but in spite of himself and his party he could not completely suppress his instinctive reformist inclinations. This was especially so once he became president. His first annual message to Congress carried a warning about the dangers of the accumulating power of the great monopolists. Roosevelt had no sympathy for attacks on capitalism as a system, and, in fact, was impressed by the drive and power of the leaders of finance and industry. It was their recklessness and excesses he despised. He railed against those he called "malefactors of great wealth," and against the influence of "plutocracy." On the other hand, he also disdained movements among the laboring classes like organized labor or the Populists. What was needed was a disinterested mediator between self-interested and contending forces for the sake of the national interest. TR had little difficulty casting himself for the part. As the political realities unfolded during his presidency and after, he tended more frequently to anger conservative and business interests to the cheers of progressive factions. Conservatives in his own party regarded Roosevelt with some distrust early on; by the time he sought to return to the White House in the 1912 presidential campaign, distrust had turned to a visceral hatred.

His analysis of the political and economic landscape moved Roosevelt from early and well-publicized anti-trust efforts to the idea of effective government oversight and action. Early in his administration he took on the Morgan, James J. Hill, and Edward H. Harriman interests in his successful prosecution of the Northern Securities railroad monopoly. That the government would challenge this huge company headed by three of the most powerful businessmen in the country stunned Wall Street. More shocking was the vigor of the prosecution and the decision of the Court to order the breakup of the monopoly. The Northern Securities case and others against Rockefeller's Standard Oil and the American Tobacco Company established Roosevelt's reputation as a trustbuster (even though Taft and Wilson after him initiated more prosecutions than did TR). More important was the precedent set that the government had some obligation to intervene in the economic life of the nation.

But breaking up the trusts, Roosevelt came to realize, was not enough. Broken trusts could reorganize and devise new strategies for market control untroubled by prosecution. The size of a corporation was not the problem in itself; corporate behavior was more troublesome. Taming corporate behavior required more regular oversight and regulation by government authority. With the support of a growing number of progressives in both parties, Roosevelt took the first effective steps toward federal regulation with measures for railroad regulation and pure food and drug laws. The Elkins Act of 1903 made railroads liable for prosecution for proffering competition-killing rebates to favored customers. After a struggle with a conservative Senate, the president won passage of the Hepburn Act assigning broad regulatory powers over railroads and other transportation facilities to the Interstate Commerce Commission. While some progressives in Congress were unhappy with compromises the president agreed to in order to get the legislation through a very conservative Senate, the Hepburn Act clearly established a new regulatory role for government in the affairs of American business.

The scope of that regulatory function soon widened. In 1906, Roosevelt championed the Meat Inspection Act and the Pure Food and Drug Act, which made an important start in safeguarding the public health against the more disgusting practices of less-than-fastidious producers. News reports of foul and dangerous practices that contaminated food and drug supplies were not uncommon, and Upton Sinclair's novel *The Jungle* effectively dramatized the fetid conditions of the meat-packing industry. Once again Roosevelt's political skill and influence buttressed by popular support pushed the legislation past reluctant conservatives in Congress and added to the government's role as custodian of the public health and welfare. Roosevelt pushed the custodial role of government still further in his determined and skillful campaign to set millions of acres of federal lands out of the reach of private interests, to the distress of industry lobbyists and congressional conservatives. With the help of Gifford Pinchot, chief of the Forest Service, Roosevelt finessed the passage of legislation that greatly expanded the national park system and awakened broad popular support of conservation in the United States.

During his presidency Theodore Roosevelt changed his once rather hostile attitude toward labor. When the nationwide coal strike of 1902 threatened to bring on a winter crisis, he brought representatives of union workers and management to the White House. That the president should intervene in this way was itself unprecedented. With some surprise, he found the union men more respectful and more reasonable in their positions than the stonily rigid management representatives. His intervention and pressure helped settle the strike.

By these and other actions Roosevelt worked important changes in the relation of the presidency and the government to the national economy. In 1912, unhappy with the course of his friend and successor, William Howard Taft, and fervently eager to return to office, Roosevelt led his Bull Moose Progressive Party on a platform that was for its day not merely progressive, but radical. He had by this time added a broad program of social reform to the earlier agenda of government action to harness capital. He campaigned with the slogan "the New Nationalism," calling for a vigorous government acting as the steward of the general welfare. To this end he endorsed ideas like an income tax, a minimum wage, protection for women and children in the workplace, workmen's compensation, old age pensions, and even, alas, a national health service. Roosevelt was influenced by the ideas of Herbert Croly, a leading progressive who wrote *The Promise of American Life*. In that book Croly rejected Jefferson's fear of government and called for strong leaders wielding sweeping federal authority to control corporate power in the interests of the common good. Croly's thoughts were not without influence, and in 1912, such ideas were hard for Theodore Roosevelt to resist.

When old-guard conservative Republicans who controlled the national convention refused to nominate Roosevelt despite a majority of primary victories and what seemed to be the support of the rank and file, he claimed their delegate selection had cheated him and bolted the party. A hastily organized Bull Moose convention roared its approval of a stem-winding Roosevelt oration laying out his reform ideas. His platform and his campaign set the standard for what came to be the liberal American response to the power of capital and the needs of the people in an industrial age. Although a young Franklin Roosevelt was a Democrat, he much admired his distant cousin and the uncle of Eleanor, and would live to champion the spirit and letter of much of TR's 1912 program.

Democrats, hungry for the presidency they had controlled for only eight years since 1860, nominated Woodrow Wilson in 1912. Like Theodore Roosevelt, Wilson was a rather conservative thinker in his youth. Even while serving as president of Princeton, Wilson became more active in political circles and entertained thoughts of public office. By 1910 he was a candidate for governor of New Jersey. Despite a lingering conservative reputation, Wilson was able to win over New Jersey progressives, pledging support for the Democratic platform that reformers had managed to push through the state party convention. He garnered more support with a series of impressive campaign speeches backing the Progressive platform. Compared to the professorial commentator who was friendly to business interests and expressed skepticism about government regulation, this was a new Wilson in 1910. He consolidated his political reputation as a progressive by leading a vigorously reformist administration as governor of New Jersey. His reorganization of state government and successful anti-corruption work drew wide national attention and quickly made Wilson a contender for the Democratic presidential nomination in 1912.

The election returns in 1912 suggested the United States was ready for dramatic political change. Bull Moose Roosevelt and Democrat Wilson spoke the language of progressivism; Socialist Eugene Debs [this election gave Socialists their best percentage ever] offered more radical solutions; and only incumbent Republican William Howard Taft defended conservative caution. The returns spoke the mood of the country. More than 11 million votes out of a total of almost 15 million were cast for the candidates who represented change; Taft finished a weak third. Despite his popularity, Roosevelt could not overcome the Republican Party split, and Woodrow Wilson became president.

Even now Wilson still harbored an outdated Jeffersonian fear of strong central government. During the campaign, his response to

Roosevelt's New Nationalism was to coin the slogan the New Freedom. Who could say how even a well-intentioned strong government would behave once in power? And if it behaved badly, how could it be dismantled once endowed with great powers? However, once faced with the demands of governing, Wilson adjusted. Wilson became an activist president leading a vigorous government. His economic and social agenda was closer to Roosevelt's inclinations than his New Freedom rhetoric had suggested. Within two years, Wilson engineered the passage of laws that provided a graduated income tax, lowered tariffs for American consumers, established the Federal Reserve System, and added muscle to the provisions of the earlier Sherman Act and exempted labor unions from anti-strike injunctions with the Clayton Anti-Trust Act. He also supported the creation of the Federal Trade Commission, the Fair Trade Act, a ban on child labor (later struck down by the Supreme Court), an eight-hour law for railroad workers, and the reform of working conditions for merchant sailors. This surge of progressive action invested the government with a new role in the economic life of the nation, confronting the demands of social justice and the realities of modern capitalism.

The work of Theodore Roosevelt and Woodrow Wilson, which began to adjust the role of government to the realities of modern economic power, was two-pronged. One aim was to police the behavior of capital through as yet very limited regulatory structures. The second pointed toward government support for improving the economic condition of the agrarian and industrial laboring masses. Both functions were new. By later standards, the actions of these two presidents were modest in achievement, but they were truly important as precedent.

Resistance to such reform was insistent. There was something dangerous and even un-American in challenging the orthodoxies of classical economics and the mythologies of self-reliance and unrestrained competition. The election of 1920 signaled a return to the more conservative comforts of the days of McKinley and the retreat of an apparently exhausted progressive movement. Richard Hofstadter has pointed out that energies once dedicated to genuine reform were now deflected toward the banning of alcohol and Darwin, and toward the primitive civic passions of the Ku Klux Klan.[1] Jazz, radio, and the movies distracted. Meanwhile, the world of business enjoyed unrestrained influence. In their wisdom, business leaders constructed an agreeable economic agenda in league with a conservative political establishment only too anxious to cooperate. Business looked for lower taxes, higher tariffs on imports, and limited union influence. During the 1920s Congress lowered taxes on the highest incomes, raised tariff rates to the highest levels, and stood firmly hostile to organized labor, whose membership fell dramatically during the decade.

The conventional economic wisdom of the American business community and its political toadies dominated the 1920s with a confidence gilded by apparent prosperity and untroubled by doubt, conscience, or serious thought. After all, the stock market confirmed the authority of the consensus almost daily. But the calculus was faulty. Keeping wages as low as possible meant that much of the industrial laboring class could not afford to buy the products they were making. Low farm prices and continuing farm foreclosures assured that farmers could not buy those products or consume much beyond the necessities and fewer even of those. What American business could not sell to workers and farmers at home, they could not sell overseas in adequate quantity because of trade barriers erected in response to the American high-tariff policies for which they had successfully lobbied. No clear voice thought to point out that new technology, massive productive capacity, relatively cheap labor, and abundant plant space could provide everything necessary for a thriving consumer economy—except consumers. The needs of the prosperous, even with the most imaginative efforts at accumulation, the economic engine could meet without strain. But when production outran demand for long enough, excess supply required that the machinery spin more slowly. The signs were there in 1928 and early 1929 even in the limited economic statistics of the day. Those numbers showed housing construction in sharp decline, inventories climbing, consumer spending down, and unemployment rising. But for the time being investors ignored the signs and remained untroubled.

The stock market of the 1920s showed the signs of a classic bubble, and sooner or later it had to burst. Sooner came in the last days of October 1929. The decade's speculation in stocks, swollen by easy credit for unregulated margin buying, reached obscene and unsustainable levels during 1929. Thus huge purchases of stock were made with only a small percentage of the cost paid in cash as buyers and brokers accumulated massive unsupported debt. During that summer, stock in companies like Westinghouse, General Electric, U.S. Steel, and American Telephone and Telegraph rose by 50 to 75 percent. The wise had left the market, some as early as 1928. By the time the less cautious saw the danger in the last days of October, they were caught by a flood of panic selling in a market without buyers. U.S. Steel, which had sold for as high as $262 in 1929, was available at $22 in July 1932. The fall was not untypical of other major corporations that eventually survived the hard times; many less robust firms, alas, did not. The market crash intensified but did not in itself cause the Great Depression. The crash was a late recognition that the economy was already in decline. The downward spiral continued, it seemed to observers, without discernable end. The Hoover administration reluctantly engineered feeble efforts to deal with the crisis, but with little effect. Hoover's civic philosophy was full of caution lest government largesse weaken the moral fiber of the needy and undermine the American spirit of self reliance. At the moment hunger threatened the decay of the physical fiber more than the morals of the needy. The intensity of want and insecurity marked indelibly the generation that lived through the Depression era; many could not shake the fearful memories even as their children and grandchildren, years later, thrived in a new age of consumption.

It is difficult early in this new century to fully appreciate the depth of despair in the United States in 1932. Unemployment figures pushing 25 percent did not account for those whose work had been cut to part-time and whose wages were down to pennies an hour. When months turned to years without measured improvement, despair added to the pain of privation and raised doubts about the future of the country. Questions about democracy itself underlay the bitter economic times. Could liberty and equality survive in a world of want? Unfettered capitalism had had its day and the result was collapse and equilibrium at the level of stagnation. The radically inclined, often aglow with perceived opportunity in times of disaster, celebrated even as they accused. Capitalism had failed, incapable of coping with modern demands. Marx was right; this was the big one from which there could be no recovery, only revolution. Democracy was finished, impotent against the complexity of modern life and the need for rapid, decisive action. Mussolini's trains ran, and ran on time. Lincoln Steffens, the aging muckraker, made a hero of Mussolini and, looking to two extremes at once, also admired what he saw as the progress made in Russia. For a band of American intellectuals, even the Socialism of Norman Thomas was mere reformism. The real answer to the failure of capitalism, they argued, was Communism.[2]

This was the condition of the United States in 1933 when a cheerful and confident Franklin Delano Roosevelt sought to rally the nation against the numbing discouragement of hard times that seemed perpetual. He set out to attack the immediate problems of economic chaos and wide-spread suffering, *and* to plan for the permanent changes in the structure of American capitalism that became the Third American Revolution.

In this task, Franklin Roosevelt completed the work begun by Theodore Roosevelt and Woodrow Wilson in adjusting the American democratic response to the realities of modern capitalist power. The work of the earlier Roosevelt and Wilson, both of whom Franklin deeply admired, was preliminary, tentative, and limited. Resistance to their efforts was dogged. The reigning economic orthodoxy insisted that there should be no interference with the mystic operation of the free market, which was inevitably beneficent and self-correcting. The system should remain especially free from government meddling. Businessmen were, of course, more practical than the philosophers of free enterprise, and were more than willing to exempt subsidies (like those that built the great railroads) and protective tariffs (long after any plausible need for protection) from classification as government meddling. But, exceptions aside, there was unanimity among the business classes and academic economists of classical faith that regulation of economic practice was, like all heresy, dangerous. Franklin Roosevelt, however, came from that progressive tradition that eventually recognized limitless economic power beyond the reach of any electorate or public authority could threaten the relevance of the democracy itself. The Depression crisis gave him the opportunity to confront the ideologues, rigid in their defense of entrenched capital, with a kind of bold experimentation in the public interest. Such would not have been congenial or possible for Theodore Roosevelt or Woodrow Wilson.

4

The Mind of FDR

Franklin Roosevelt is often described as a pragmatist who responded to emergency conditions with sometimes conflicting experiments but without roots in a political philosophy or ideology. For example, even friendly historians like Frank Freidel and Arthur Schlesinger saw little ideological coherence in the New Deal. Freidel acknowledged an admiration for cousin Theodore's vigorous governance and a progressive optimism in FDR, but found it difficult to identify a clear ideology. Schlesinger saw the New Deal as distinguished by "its refusal to approach social problems in terms of ideology."[1] Others have joined in describing the New Deal as inconsistent and even contradictory, having little ideological coherence.[2] It has been argued that there was "no evidence of a coherent and consistent set of principles from which Roosevelt was operating." One biographer describes him as a marvelous "paradox: a practical idealist."[3] But Roosevelt's pragmatic and often shifting responses to Depression problems were not, as often claimed, without an underlying political philosophy. Partial truth draws a distorted portrait. There was a moral and political coherence in Roosevelt's desire, often expressed, to provide basic security and liberation from dire want for Americans. His friend and labor secretary, Frances Perkins, tells the story of a reporter asking Roosevelt about his economic philosophy. He responded, "Philosophy? I am a Christian and a Democrat—that's all." Perkins comments, "He was willing to do experimentally whatever was necessary to promote the Golden Rule and other ideals he considered to be Christian. . . ." The response, Perkins notes, never made it into the reporter's paper.[4] Roosevelt's Christian imperatives operated within the liberal, progressive ideology that he embraced as a young man.

Roosevelt was indeed experimental, consciously so. "The country needs and, unless I mistake its temper, the country demands bold, persistent experimentation. It is common sense to take a method and try it: if it fails, admit it frankly and try another. But above all try something."[5] He did contradict himself; he came into office from a campaign that looked toward a balanced budget, and his policies in office often ran counter to his basic commitment to classical economic doctrine. His flexibility made possible a nimble response to the stubborn crisis. Roosevelt was able to distinguish between those rare occasions when a stand on principle is necessary to one's integrity or a defense of high justice, and the more common practical demand for compromise. Herbert Hoover elevated conventional economic and political ideas to the plane of hallowed principle with unflinching tenacity even as the economy crumbled and the nation suffered. Statesmen of such dedicated conviction often do much damage.

From childhood in Hyde Park to the day of his first inauguration, a convergence of influences shaped Franklin Roosevelt's moral and political posture. Two figures much revered by Roosevelt were his father, James, and Endicott Peabody, headmaster of Groton. From them he absorbed the lesson he would one day preach to the nation that everyone is responsible for everyone else.[6] From both he drew a deep sense of social obligation as a religious imperative. James Roosevelt continued the family tradition of involvement in a variety of business enterprises successfully enough to provide a most comfortable and genteel life for his family among the gentry of Dutchess County. Although James was a grandfatherly 54 years old when Franklin was born, the two were very close. He gave a great deal of time and attention to his son, and they were virtual playmates as he attended to the Hyde Park estate and taught young Franklin much about the land, its cultivation, and its conservation. His example and instruction were also evident in repeated family tours of Europe. During his campaign for the state assembly in 1910, Franklin told a Hyde Park audience who knew his father that it was his wish to follow his father's model.[7]

James Roosevelt died in 1900, but Peabody remained important to Roosevelt for many years. He understood that paramount to his role at Groton was the development of religious commitment and a sense of Christian duty in its students. Peabody hovered over every detail of the school he founded, especially the boys' instruction and discipline. He exhorted his charges with the precepts of a muscular Christianity prescribing charitable concern for the good of society. He regularly addressed the students in chapel, offering a kind of social gospel that stressed public service as a matter of religious obligation. Roosevelt never lost touch with Peabody. He presided at his marriage to Eleanor, and at Roosevelt's request conducted services at St. John's Episcopal Church in Lafayette Square on the morning of his inaugurations in 1933 and 1937. Somewhat conservative in politics for most of his life, Peabody came around to support Roosevelt's New Deal policies. As president, the Groton alumnus reminded Peabody of one of his school sermons admonishing students not to abandon their ideals as they grew older. "Those were Groton ideals—taught by you—I try not to forget—and your words are still with me."[8] Sending a greeting to Peabody on his 84th birthday in 1941, FDR told his old mentor that he considered himself blessed to have spent his formative years under his guidance.[9]

Religious commitment was important to his political outlook and ultimately to the cast of his social revolution. One of his Brain Trust advisers said Roosevelt believed he was doing God's work.[10] Roosevelt often read the Bible and quoted from the Anglican Book of Common Prayer. He attended church services regularly when in residence at Hyde Park, but less so in Washington because of the lack of privacy. Roosevelt left little evidence of theological or doctrinal sophistication, but he was acutely conscious of the importance of religious experience. He felt strengthened by prayer and testified to a connection with God as a real part of his life.[11] He referred to religion quite naturally and drew from religious ideas about improving the human condition. Eleanor Roosevelt, who embraced an intensely Christian identity in her own work, testified about the importance of his faith to his self-confidence, helping him through difficult decisions without hand-wringing self-doubt. "He believed in God and his guidance." All this was very personal and largely private; he seldom spoke of his personal religious beliefs. Frances Perkins, who worked so closely with him for years in social and labor reform, said, "He saw the betterment of life and people as part of God's work, and felt that man's devotion to God expressed itself by serving his fellow man."[12] In a revealing moment on a train to Washington for his inauguration, Roosevelt's thoughts turned to religion, which, he said in conversation with his campaign manager, Jim Farley, "will be the means of bringing us out of the depths of despair into which so many have apparently fallen."[13]

His concern for others was manifest even during his brief life as a practicing lawyer. In that work he often took small claims cases of people in difficult straits and learned to deal comfortably on behalf of the common man.[14] That concern became political when he was elected to the New York State Senate in 1910 with the encouragement of cousin Theodore, despite their party difference. In Albany, he joined young, reform-minded senators like Al Smith and Robert Wagner, forming a group of about 20 senators who resolved to fight Tammany Hall domination of the Democratic Party.

It was during these political squabbles that he came to the attention of Louis Howe, then a reporter in Albany for the *New York Herald*. Howe eventually became Roosevelt's most trusted policy advisor, critic, and campaign aide, and with single-minded devotion spent the rest of his life promoting the ambitions and success of his friend and patron. An excellent reporter and astute political observer and analyst, Howe spotted Roosevelt as presidential material in the earliest days of his Albany battles with the Tammany bosses and the Republicans in the legislature. In Roosevelt's fight to block the Tammany-picked candidate for the U. S. Senate [senators were still chosen by state legislatures], Howe wrote high praise for the freshman legislator taking on the machine. A permanent connection was cemented in 1912 when Roosevelt became ill with typhoid fever at the start of his campaign for reelection to the New York Senate. Howe abandoned newspaper work and took control of the campaign as Roosevelt's proxy, organizing mailings and campaign advertising. Roosevelt was reelected with a larger vote than in his first election and even outpolled Woodrow Wilson in his district.

From the start, Howe was confident Roosevelt would one day be president of the United States, and he was determined to make it happen. With his sharp understanding of policy formation, political strategy, partisan infighting, public opinion, and timing, Howe proved invaluable to Roosevelt's rise to political prominence and power. The chain-smoking and sartorially indifferent Howe won over an initially unfriendly Eleanor Roosevelt and became virtually a member of the family, frequently in residence at Hyde Park and other Roosevelt homes, and living in the White House itself during the last years of his life. This intimate personal and political association lasted until Howe's death in 1936.

Moving into national politics with Howe always close, Roosevelt enthusiastically supported Woodrow Wilson in 1912, by which time his progressive posture was clearly evident. He still greatly admired cousin Theodore and applauded his revolt against the old-guard Republicans, but he was a Democrat and Wilson was his leader and held the promise of a future in the party. He warmly endorsed Wilson's reform ideas in the campaign and later as part of the administration. This he could do with vigor because he had admired Theodore Roosevelt's transformation of the role of government in national life and believed that the New Nationalism of TR and Wilson's New Freedom could be reconciled. In support of Wilson he argued that competition was productive, but a good society required cooperation—a broader concern for the common good.[15] In Roosevelt's political thought and action it was an enduring idea.

The reward for his support for Wilson was the appointment he coveted as assistant secretary of the Navy, the post that had been held by a young Theodore Roosevelt under William McKinley. Roosevelt was only 31 when he took his new post, and his political education continued in Washington as a member of the Wilson administration and in the larger social circle of the city. He joined the Common Counsel Club, a group of the politically interested who were dedicated to progressive ideas. He could not do without his political mentor, and he brought Louis Howe to Washington as his aide. The assistant secretary greatly enjoyed the perks of office and gained valuable political experience and skill in dealing with tough-skinned naval officers and with the hard-shelled congressmen who had to be courted for appropriations. Roosevelt had frequent contact with President Wilson on Navy Department matters, and developed great respect for the president and for his program of reform.

Active involvement in naval affairs did not discourage Roosevelt from toying with the idea of a run for governor of New York or for a seat in the U. S. Senate. Tammany Hall stood in the path to both, but he did enter the primary for the Senate race in 1914, losing by a large margin. Tammany boss Charles F. Murphy made it particularly difficult for Roosevelt by backing the candidacy of James Gerard, a scrupulously honest and distinguished ambassador to Germany. A difficult opponent, poor timing, and the complexities of New York Democratic politics all worked against Roosevelt's bid. The result was an overwhelming primary victory for Gerard. The effort taught a memorable lesson in practical politics; FDR would not again challenge Tammany leadership head-on.

During his years with Wilson, Roosevelt warmly supported the president's progressive policies and came to a greater appreciation of the role of government in solving national problems. He also gave his full commitment to Wilson's idea for the League of Nations, though in later years his enthusiasm waned. But in 1920 he supported American entry into the League even after Wilson's defeat on the issue in the Senate. That support, the Roosevelt name, and a record of good service in the Navy department made him a candidate for vice president in that election year. Roosevelt had mended fences with Tammany forces and the old hostility had been replaced by tolerance if not cordiality by the time of the Democratic convention in San Francisco late in June. One sign of better relations: Roosevelt was asked and quickly agreed to place the name of Al Smith in nomination as a New York favorite son and as a gesture in support of Smith's real candidacy for governor of the state. In the serious contest for the nomination, Roosevelt favored William G. McAdoo, secretary of the treasury and Wilson's son-in-law. In the end the convention broke in favor of James Cox, governor of Ohio. The disappointment of the McAdoo loss turned to opportunity for Roosevelt. Looking to take advantage of the Roosevelt name and also seeing the benefit of joining with a McAdoo supporter and member of the Wilson administration, Cox sent out the word that he wanted Franklin as his running mate. No blocking maneuver came from Tammany forces who had supported Cox after their gesture toward Smith.

In a losing cause, Roosevelt campaigned around the country, loyal to Cox, Wilson's League idea, and a progressive domestic agenda. It was a tough sell. Wilson had lost his long struggle for ratification of the Versailles Treaty with its provision for a League of Nations, during which he suffered debilitating strokes. The president was disabled and the issue was effectively dead. The war and the League issue disrupted progressive unity, and enthusiasm for more reform wilted. Warren Harding better reflected the will of the electorate, apparently tired of both war and reform. The next three administrations of Harding, Coolidge, and Hoover prepared the way for economic disaster.

During the summer after the election, Franklin, Eleanor, and the children enjoyed their favorite summer retreat at Campobello. In the second week of August, Roosevelt fell ill with what was diagnosed as polio. Hope for quick improvement soon turned into anxiety about his survival. By the time the danger of death passed, paralysis had set in. Despite years of heroic effort to regain mobility, Roosevelt remained a permanent invalid. Even as it assaulted his body, his illness seemed to reinforce qualities of character and temperament already present. He confronted his disability with stoic determination and refused to complain or feel sorry for himself. One close observer of Roosevelt was convinced that he had undergone a kind of spiritual conversion during his illness. Frances Perkins saw in him more humility, a strengthening of religious faith, and a greater inner serenity. And his own hard times seemed to intensify his sensitivity to people in trouble and to the suffering of others.[16] Eleanor, too, saw a growth in strength of will and courage as he confronted his illness with remarkable patience and undiscouraged persistence. All of these qualities served usefully in the years of political struggle ahead; rather than destroy his future, the illness ironically toughened and prepared him for the rigors of a public life.

After months of recuperation, that public life beckoned again. With encouragement from Eleanor and the insistence of the ever-supportive Louis Howe, the Roosevelt name drew the attention of press and public. Howe refused to reconcile to the idea that Roosevelt's political career was over. He and Eleanor grew close in this period as partners in their work to sustain Franklin as an active political presence. This deviated sharply from Sara Roosevelt's expressed desire that her son retire to Hyde Park and the quiet life of a disabled country gentleman.

In 1922, Roosevelt broadcast his support for Al Smith's bid to return to the governorship after his defeat in the Republican landslide of 1920. Although they never became warm friends, Smith and Roosevelt appreciated the value of mutual support at key moments during this decade. Eleanor and Louis Howe represented Franklin at the state convention cheering for Smith and keeping a Roosevelt presence in party affairs. She campaigned for Smith and worked hard to get out the vote in Dutchess County. At Howe's urging, Eleanor continued her political activity after the election. She was important in establishing the women's division of the Democratic party in New York, and before long she established herself as a political operative in her own right. She became Franklin's eyes and voice in the party. She traveled the state, helped to sustain Franklin's political network, and returned to him with valuable party intelligence.

When Smith decided on a run for the presidency in 1924, he asked FDR to head his campaign and then to place his name in nomination at the Democratic convention. In an electrifying moment in American political history, Roosevelt, on crutches, struggled to the podium for the nominating speech to the wild cheers of the assembled delegates. The nomination went to John W. Davis, who made a quixotic effort to outdo the Republicans in fulsome commitment to conservatism. It was a losing strategy.

During the mid-twenties, Roosevelt held no elective office, but he maintained an active correspondence with party leaders in New York and across the country, positioning himself for future possibilities. In 1928, he again nominated Smith for president at the Democratic convention, this time with success. With a masterful "happy warrior" speech on behalf of Smith, Roosevelt electrified the convention and did no harm to his own image as a party leader. A grateful Smith, in turn, supported Roosevelt's nomination to be his successor as governor of New York. This was more than gratitude, for Smith needed New York's vote if he hoped to win the presidency and Roosevelt on the ballot would surely help. That Roosevelt would run was not a foregone conclusion. His first response to Smith was to decline. Louis Howe thought the timing was not right and opposed the idea; Eleanor, too, was reluctant. In the end, Roosevelt gave in to pressure from Smith and the call of party duty. The Democratic state convention nominated Roosevelt by acclamation.

At the national level, the American electorate seemed serenely content with what passed for Republican "normalcy" in 1928, and Hoover swamped Smith in November. It is often noted that Smith was at a great disadvantage as the first Roman Catholic nominee of a major party. There is some truth in this. Anti-Catholic prejudice had not disappeared in American society and would persist in some ways for decades longer. Indeed, the issue whether a Catholic should be a candidate for the presidency was raised again as late as 1960 concerning John F. Kennedy. The rising membership of the Ku Klux Klan in the 1920s was in part a reflection of the prejudice as the Klan focused its venom on blacks, Catholics, and Jews. It is true that his Catholicism cost Smith some votes normally cast in the Democratic column. Heavily Protestant Southern states like Virginia, North and South Carolina, Texas, Florida, Tennessee, and Kentucky abandoned their established pattern of the Democratic "Solid South" and gave their majorities to Republican Hoover. Nevertheless, his Catholicism alone did not cost Smith the election. He was the wrong candidate at the wrong time. In an election when radio was now playing a significant role, he spoke in the twangy tones of the streets of the East Side of New York in contrast to Hoover's midwestern "standard" American English. Smith was a wet; Hoover was a dry, an important difference to rural and southern Americans. Smith was easily associated with Tammany Hall politics; Hoover projected an all-American image of success in humanitarian and business ventures. Probably most important to Hoover's victory was the apparent prosperity and promise of the decade. The diseases eating into the economy were not yet recognized, and there seemed little reason to set a new political direction.

In New York, years of solid support for Smith as governor benefited his designated successor, so despite the Hoover landslide, Roosevelt won a narrow victory against the national trend. His opponent was conservative Republican Albert Ottinger, the honest and well-respected attorney general of the state. Roosevelt smothered his doubts about running and gathered an effective team for what all knew would be an uphill struggle. Joining the battle were people who would stay with Roosevelt and be important to him as governor and in the White House. Frances Perkins was there and would serve him in industrial relations as governor and become his secretary of labor in Washington. Samuel I. Rosenman prepared issue statements for the candidate, who often reworked the ideas for greater punch and vitality. Rosenman was impressed, learned the tricks, and became Roosevelt's principal speechwriter for years. James A. Farley, so important to the victory in 1932 and later postmaster general, ran the New York City headquarters of the campaign. These were the people FDR called on to shape the character of his administration.

To bury questions from the opposition, the press, and the public about his physical ability to do the job of governor, Roosevelt campaigned with untiring vigor by train and automobile aiming at maximum visibility and contact with voters across the state. Even the unenthusiastic conceded Roosevelt was a great campaigner who managed to make something of an aristocratic bearing appealing to the ordinary citizen. The full measure of Roosevelt magic was needed to bring home the prize. He survived the Republican tidal wave, but barely. The margin of victory came to 25,000 votes out of a total of over four million cast.

Bitter about his decisive loss in the presidential election, Al Smith apparently hoped to retreat to New York to guide the administration of his successor from the sidelines. Even as governor-elect Roosevelt was forced to resist Smith's repeated attempts to direct his personnel and policy decisions, and he made clear from the start that he would strike an independent course without Smith as power behind the throne. He also quickly demonstrated his political talent—establishing an effective administration, dealing with a hostile legislature, and communicating with his constituents. As governor he developed what would be so useful to him as president: regular radio chats to explain complex policy decisions in clear language without condescension.

Roosevelt's return to active political life in New York said something about the evolution of his progressive thought and even forecast some of his presidential policies. In a key campaign address in Buffalo in October, he struck at Republican conservatism, particularly in its icy attitude toward labor, and stood firmly on the Democratic state platform. One plank argued for legislation to limit the use of injunctions in labor disputes and others advocated old-age pensions, minimum wage laws for women and children, and the extension of workmen's compensation benefits. The platform also called for a declaration in law that human labor should not be treated as a commodity. Roosevelt warned the crowd that his conservative "friends" would greet the proposal for old-age pensions, for example, using words like "Red," "radical," and "socialistic." But he reminded the audience that modest reform ideas like workmen's compensation and factory inspection were so labeled only a few years earlier. In the 1920s charges of radicalism were made easily and often against politicians of progressive intent, an enduring habit in American politics. The next day in Queens, Roosevelt noted the charge of "socialism" Herbert Hoover leveled against the record of Al Smith as governor of New York. With a clip of ironic humor that he would use repeatedly in the future, Roosevelt listed reduction of work hours for women and children, improvement of state hospitals and prisons, aid to education, and improved public parks among Smith's achievements. If these were socialist, he said, "We are all socialists."[17]

Roosevelt maintained much of the tone and substance of the campaign in his first annual message to the legislature in January. His menu for action included an eight-hour day and 48-hour week for women and children, establishment of a minimum wage board, an emergency rent law, as well as those positions on injunctions, pensions, and workmen's compensation mentioned in his speech at Buffalo. The focus of these ideas was assistance to people, not simply fidelity to an ideology of moderate reform. This agenda would be overshadowed later in the year by the stock market collapse and the inexorable sinking into the Great Depression, but a similar list he later revived and incorporated as part of the response to Depression pain. During the years FDR was governor, New York did more for its people than the federal government through the state's strong and active departments of health, education, and public welfare. But Roosevelt became increasingly convinced that the limited tax bases and resources of a state were not adequate to the demands of the day, and the federal government had to be more active. "Any Nation worthy of the name should aim in normal industrial periods to offer employment to every able-bodied citizen willing to work," he said, and added that unemployment insurance should be provided for the hard times. Speaking at the national Governors Conference in 1931, he raised the question why government should not do more to help citizens in a disaster. Roosevelt's political outlook was deeply influenced by the felt obligation to help people in need and the recognition that modern conditions required government agency in providing that help. He carried into his campaign for the presidency the idea that the federal government must bear a responsibility for human welfare.[18]

For Roosevelt, this was not a new idea. In June 1929, four months before the start of the Wall Street collapse, Governor Roosevelt delivered the Phi Beta Kappa address at Harvard during the 25th reunion celebration of his graduating class. Written in his own hand, the speech—especially in its conclusion—clearly revealed the trajectory of his political and social thought.[19] The talk was something of a tour de force as FDR delivered a mini-history and analysis of the development of Western civilization. He reviewed with intelligence and sophistication the travails and progress of society from the Greeks to modern times. He offered special praise for the scientific, educational, and technological progress of the 19th century. Turning his focus on the still young 20th century, he thought it best described as the "Age of Social Consciousness." It was a time of "the very definite breaking down of the remnants of hereditary cast. . . ." He noted the clear advance in the quality of life of ordinary people and celebrated the collapse of artificial barriers among people and the steadily egalitarian movement of society.

The praise was accompanied by a warning about the "glaring instances of individual or group selfishness, dishonesty in high places, and, of late, a tendency toward the concentration of material power in the hands of the few" and cautioned against the danger of oligarchy in the future. Supporting evidence for these phenomena during the decade of the 1920s was not scarce. Nevertheless, he argued that the nation's heightened social consciousness had encouraged a keener sense of community obligation than in the past through government, religious, and private initiatives. He believed this stronger social consciousness conformed "more truly to the teachings of religion" and advised embracing and directing this social consciousness, guided by traditional moral imperatives, for the improvement of society. The very definition of the term "My Neighbor" was changing and now applied "far more to fellow men and women, rich and poor, Jew and Gentile, than it did in the days gone by" when the term was more narrowly confined to one's personal associates.

Here were clear expressions of the elements of a progressive political philosophy shaped in his youth, honed by his religious understanding and his political experience, and which would later inform his response to the Depression crisis. His thought and eventually his policies were moved by a vision of fraternal and communal responsibility as imperatives for both individuals and governments.

Even before the Depression crisis struck, Roosevelt launched a sturdily progressive administration. He called for a program of tax relief for hard-pressed farmers who were suffering even before the collapse of the national economy. He set Frances Perkins to work to investigate solutions to the problem of old-age security. He proposed stiffer regulation of electric rates and explored the possibility of establishing public power projects, which could serve as guides and restraints on private utilities. In the tradition of Theodore and following his own lifelong inclinations he pressed for conservation measures, including a program of reforestation.

Roosevelt's performance as governor drew national attention and applause. New York's attack on Depression hardship under his administration was among the most effective in the country and in sharp contrast with the anemic response from Washington. Frances Perkins gathered data to confirm the intensity of the unemployment problem and suggested immediate and long-term solutions for the problem. The centerpiece of the New York effort against unemployment and poverty was the Temporary Emergency Relief Administration (TERA) established in 1931 with Harry Hopkins as its administrator. Hopkins entered the field of social work as a young man and worked at a settlement house on New York's East Side, headed the city Bureau of Child Welfare in 1915, and later joined the Red Cross and other social work organizations. Hopkins's appointment began one of the most important associations of Roosevelt's political life. He became the most brilliant and effective of Roosevelt's New Deal administrators and a trusted confidant of the president on many issues. Over its life TERA offered assistance to millions of New Yorkers during the most painful years of the Depression.[20] Despite a conservative Republican legislature, "No governor in the nation was more responsive to the challenge of the Depression."[21]

The people of New York approved of Roosevelt's performance with his reelection in 1930. He successfully fended off trouble from a new burst of Tammany Hall scandals in New York City and stood on his record of early response to the economic emergency. The result was impressive. Roosevelt defeated his Republican opponent, Charles Tuttle, with a landslide 63 percent of the vote, winning big even in traditionally Republican upstate counties. Roosevelt's leadership in New York drew such wide national notice that it sparked quick interest in a possible presidential candidacy for 1932.

The maturing of a political ideology is not a quick process but stretches over time and experience. The examples of Theodore Roosevelt and Woodrow Wilson are instructive. Theodore Roosevelt was an insistent and fervent Republican Party loyalist with deeply conservative instincts during much of his New York political career. He impatiently dismissed progressive types as "do-gooders," and once, perhaps exaggerating to make a point, said he thought the Populist champions of reform would have to be confronted at the barricades of revolution. Thoughtful experience on the streets and in the politics of the city and state of New York and confrontations with the power of arrogant capital during his presidency eventually dissolved his conservative rigidities. In New York his friend Jacob Riis, among others, offered TR instruction on how the other *nine-tenths* lived. As noted, during the threatened nationwide coal strike in 1902, a stunned Roosevelt discovered miners' union representatives more receptive to reasoned argument and compromise than representatives of management. Perhaps it should not have taken him so long to learn that unions were not dangerous incubators of revolution, but learn he did. He also witnessed big business exploitation and waste of federally owned natural resources, indifference to conservation, and corruption of the nation's food and drug supplies. The result was a political transformation. The Bull Moose Roosevelt of the 1912 campaign was a different animal altogether.

Woodrow Wilson moderated the conservative views of his Princeton days during his quest for the governorship of New Jersey in 1910. After leading a reform administration in that state he was, by 1912, a progressive candidate for president on a reform platform of the New Freedom, different in temper but not drastically different in detail from Roosevelt's New Nationalism. In the early years of his presidency he won the passage of a progressive agenda including reforms in banking, lower tariffs, a progressive income tax, anti-trust laws, and pro-labor legislation. Eventually he overcame earlier reluctance drawn from a Southern gentleman's chivalric notion of femininity and supported the women's suffrage amendment. By 1916, with the

Republican Party dominated by conservatives uncongenial to those who had bolted, Wilson brought to his camp many of TR's 1912 Bull Moose supporters.

Franklin Roosevelt did not have as far to travel as the first Roosevelt or Wilson. He came to political maturity in the Progressive era, and his ideas were shaped by his humane instincts, his admiration for TR, and his service in the Wilson administration. He once described his own New Deal as a combination of the New Nationalism and the New Freedom.[22] But he was not entirely free of the reigning conservative prejudices of the day. He remained tied to traditional economic theory well into his presidency, especially in its devotion to balanced budgets. He detested the deficits necessary to fight the worst of the Depression, and in 1937 tried to balance the federal budget too soon and with damaging results. Always flexible, he was moved to bold action again by economic recession and increase in unemployment. He made a quick return to the Keynesian ideas pushed by his aides, but about which he remained a skeptic. Roosevelt also harbored the fear common among the affluent that doling relief funds to the impoverished without proportionate labor on their part would damage the recipients, a thought never abandoned by the faithfully conservative. To his credit, Roosevelt did not raise these concerns to the level of stony principle. The intensity of the Depression and his own humane character moved him first to practical emergency experiments, and then his progressive political faith turned him to thoughts of long-term, systemic reform.

Eleanor Roosevelt played an important role in influencing FDR's thinking and tactics. Again she acted as the president's eyes and ears. When he was stuck in Washington, she frequently toured the country returning with insights about both politics and public opinion. She conferred with her husband regularly on policy matters, frequently pulling and tugging him in her even more liberal direction. While their political sympathies did not actually differ greatly, he was constrained by the realities of politics and the legislative process, and this she understood. Theirs was an interesting and fruitful partnership, which the president valued.

By 1935, there was measurable but painfully slow improvement in the economic condition of the country. Discouraged by business resistance and hostility that only grew stronger, Roosevelt now began to shift his focus away from solutions that demanded cooperation from an increasingly obdurate business establishment to structural changes in the relationship of the government to its citizens. From his days as governor and the earliest days of his presidential administration his thoughts ran toward a social system that would insure against some of the hardships of old age, disability, and unemployment.[23] Through his own words one can trace the growth of his thought into what became the ideology of his revolution. American individualism had become distorted from its real meaning: equal opportunity and freedom from exploitation. In a message on unemployment to an extraordinary session of the New York legislature in August 1931, he began by asking, "What is the State?" It is, he said, a human creation for mutual protection and well-being, and the government is simply the machinery through which those ends are achieved. In a campaign address in Detroit in October 1932, he called the mal-distribution of wealth and income a violation of both religious ethics and economic good sense because it did not provide the purchasing power to the mass of people as demanded by a consumer economy in an age of mass production.[24]

Central to Roosevelt's idea of democracy was the notion of community. He identified community responsibility for general welfare and the preservation of the freedom and dignity of the individual. Through the New Deal, he thought, ordinary people should "be dealt better cards to play with."[25] It was not bread alone that was at stake. "It is a moral as well as an economic question. . . . We want the opportunity to live in comfort, reasonable comfort, out of which we may build spiritual values."[26] To Congress in June 1934, he said people "want some safeguard against misfortunes which cannot be wholly eliminated in this man-made world of ours." He cited "three great objectives—the security of the home, the security of livelihood, and the security of social insurance—[as] a minimum of the promise that we can offer to the American people." And by executive order he created a Committee on Economic Security to study the problem and propose solutions.[27]

Emergency measures of the New Deal were concerned with basic elements of subsistence, meeting the immediate need for food and shelter. Roosevelt also thought in terms of a standard of living that could provide a measure of comfort and security. In 1934, in one of the free-wheeling press conferences he enjoyed, he spoke of slum clearance and getting people into decent homes. But poor people, even those with jobs, generally could not afford mortgage payments, and private capital could not risk loans to those marginally capable of making payments. Here was a role for government. "So what we are trying to do is to put up houses where these people can go in and where, because of much lower monthly payments, there is a chance of getting the money back. Private capital cannot do it. . . . Government only can do it." This was to be government activity in an area in which private capital did not want to enter.[28]

After a sweeping victory in congressional elections in November 1934, Roosevelt spoke in his annual message in January about a mandate to shift the nation's energies so that families might enjoy "a proper security, a reasonable leisure, and a decent living throughout life . . . an ambition to be preferred to the appetite for great wealth and great power."[29] That message remained consistent throughout his presidency even as he won some battles and lost others, and the message resonated with the people. In his great landslide reelection in 1936, only Maine and Vermont dissented. No candidate for the presidency since George Washington had ever come close to such a sweep. He celebrated that victory in a powerful second inaugural in praise of democracy. In an era of growing authoritarianism, he saw a challenge to democracy itself in the millions of Americans without the necessities of life. Noting the 150th anniversary of the Constitutional Convention, he argued that the founders created a stronger government expressly to "promote the general welfare." He railed against private autocratic economic powers who thought themselves privileged beyond regulation, who were now being brought into proper subordination to the democratic process. "We have always known that heedless self-interest was bad morals; we know now that it is bad economics." Progress against the Depression was visible, but more was needed. "I see one-third of a nation ill housed, ill-clad, ill-nourished." "The test of our progress is not whether we add more to the abundance of those who have too much; it is whether we provide enough for those who have too little." He spoke of erecting an enduring structure of social justice for future generations.[30]

By the late 1930s, foreign policy questions increasingly occupied FDR's attention, and of course, the war years ended the Depression and absorbed the energies of the nation and the president. But the philosophy of social justice was not abandoned even as the Congress retreated to a more conservative formation. During the campaign for reelection in 1940, the president spoke of the "counter offensive against the American people's march of social progress. It is not opposition that comes necessarily from wickedness–it is an opposition that comes from subconscious resistance to any measure that disturbs the position of privilege."[31] As late as January 1944, looking to a post-war world in his State of the Union message to Congress, Roosevelt proclaimed a "Second

Bill of Rights." Most of the message was, as expected, devoted to the war and world conditions, but he exhorted the Congress to act on the needs of Americans at home. Individual freedom demanded economic security and independence, he argued, and listed his economic Bill of Rights to "be established for all—regardless of station, race, or creed." In addition to the right to a job and a decent pay, he listed the right of farm families to a decent living, the right of small business to be free of unfair competition from monopolies, the right of every family to a decent home, the right to medical care, the right to a good education, and "the right to adequate protection from economic fears of old age, sickness, accident and unemployment."[32] The idea of a bill of economic rights became the basis of the domestic side of his 1944 campaign for reelection.

This was the philosophical context of his revolution, and the message remained essentially consistent from the Hundred Days to the end of his presidency. On the record of the New Deal, historian Richard Hofstadter expressed astonishment at the bitterness of the enemies Roosevelt made. "Nothing that Roosevelt had done warranted the vituperation he soon got in the conservative press or the obscenities that the hate-Roosevelt maniacs were bruiting about in their clubs and dining rooms. Quite understandably he began to feel that the people who were castigating him were muddle-headed ingrates." Such castigation continued to the end of his presidency and even beyond among conservatives who could never get past the myth of their own creation—that Roosevelt had destroyed something essential in American society.[33]

5

The Third Revolution—Phase I

Republican domination of the American electorate in presidential elections since 1860, upset only briefly by Cleveland and Wilson, came to an end in 1932. Louis Howe had marked Roosevelt for the presidency years earlier in the legislative halls of Albany. The Roosevelt name, success in the governorship of New York confirmed by a landslide reelection in 1930, and the opportunity presented by Hoover's identification with the economic collapse all pointed to the possibility of an electoral upheaval. While Roosevelt was now a popular and familiar name in America, the two-thirds rule for nomination in the Democratic Party was a huge hurdle.

James Farley and Howe began laying plans almost immediately after the 1930 reelection to the governorship. The gregarious Farley was state party chairman and had already proven himself a highly skilled political operative. In early summer 1931, after a planning session with the governor, Farley took advantage of an Elks convention scheduled for Seattle to set out on a reconnaissance tour of 18 states as he traveled to and from the convention. He returned with optimistic assessments of Roosevelt's strength across the country—perhaps too optimistic. The hoped-for nomination on the first ballot proved ephemeral. Since Roosevelt became governor, disagreements, small and large, had strained relations with Al Smith. Now Smith wanted another chance to run for president and thought he deserved it. But with a real chance for victory this time, the risk for the party was too great. Smith was bitter that Roosevelt had not recognized his prior claim to the nomination and hoped a deadlocked convention might yet turn to him. On the first ballot, Roosevelt led all candidates and stood far ahead of second-place Smith. On the fourth ballot, after Farley held out the prospect of a vice presidential nomination, John Nance Garner released the Texas delegation, setting off a stampede across the two-thirds barrier, and Roosevelt won the nomination.[1] The election was easier.

Despite his New York record and national popularity, Roosevelt did not inspire enthusiasm among the political pundits of the day. In his campaign for nomination and election he often spoke in generalities. Along with most academic and business economists, he was still wedded to the tradition of classical economic theory and criticized Hoover's failure to keep a balanced budget. Given Hoover's growing unpopularity, election victory seemed assured; risking offense with excessive detail was not politically prudent. Roosevelt struck what became a persistent theme of the campaign and his presidency in a radio address from Albany in April. Casting himself as a spokesman for the common man, he called on the nation to restore its faith "in the forgotten man at the bottom of the economic pyramid."[2] While the candidate drew admiring crowds, the campaign did not play well with the analysts. Walter Lippmann, often quoted as a sage then and since despite a substantial record of poor judgment, thought Roosevelt unqualified for the office. Similar dismissal came from liberal commentators like Elmer Davis, Heywood Broun, and critic Edmund Wilson. Journals on the left like the *New Republic* and the *Nation* doubted his intellectual qualifications for the presidency.[3]

The campaign for the presidency may not have offered a definitive picture of the candidate's promise as a leader (campaigns seldom do), but in the fight for nomination and election were embedded hints about Roosevelt's governing style and his political ideology. "The country needs and, unless I mistake its temper, the country demands bold, persistent experimentation. It is common sense to take a method and try it: if it fails, admit it frankly and try another. But above all, try something."[4] To a frightened nation the words resonated, as did his Chicago nomination acceptance promise of a "new deal" for the American people (although neither Roosevelt nor his advisors realized the power of that phrase until it was picked up by the press). Americans want work, he said, work which would give them a sense of dignity and security. The shape of that new deal was forecast in his Commonwealth Club Address in San Francisco in September. It was a bold statement that marked a division between a milder beginning to the campaign and a more aggressive posture thereafter.[5] The speech lamented the increasing concentration of unrestrained economic power in few hands and called for limits "on the operations of the speculator, the manipulator, even the financier . . . not to hamper individualism but to protect it." Such restraint he dubbed the duty of government on behalf of the public interest. He noted that business interests had insisted that government not interfere with private enterprise, but they had never been reluctant to accept tariff protection and other assistance. He rued the passing of genuine equal opportunity and asserted that every citizen had "a right to life; and that means that he has also a right to make a comfortable living." This was the obligation of government. In retrospect, the Commonwealth Club Address can be read as a forecast of New Deal ideology.

As he had as governor and as he would with the Fireside Chats when in the White House, Roosevelt used radio effectively in his campaign. At Detroit on October 2, he had high praise for the papal encyclical *Quadragesimo Anno* and quoted it extensively on the evils of the concentration of economic power in the hands of the few. This document was a tribute by Pius XI to the encyclical *Rerum Novarum* that Pope Leo XIII published in 1891. Leo and Pius were critics of uncontrolled capitalism and argued briefs for the rights of labor generating great distress among economically conservative Catholics and others of like disposition. These statements served as a kind of Catholic social gospel. With wise political caution the speech also quoted a leading rabbi and a Protestant document on economic justice. In a radio address from the Executive Mansion in Albany on October 13, he outlined a new role for government when he argued that "all phases of public health and welfare" were a proper concern of the federal government.[6] Clearly, his election would mean the role of government in the United States was about to change. That was precisely what worried Herbert Hoover.

In 1922 Hoover published *American Individualism,* attributing American economic and social progress to a vibrant individualism unimpeded by intrusive government. The essay warned against the dangers of radicalism lumping together everything from Communism to misguided proposals for increased government regulation of business practices. During the campaign President Hoover and the Republicans insisted that any deviation from the "sound economic principles" of traditional definition would only make the current troubles worse. Hoover believed and told the voters that electing Roosevelt was certain to bring radicalism amounting to revolution to the nation. Resorting to a tactic that has become standard in the political repertoire of the

archly conservative, he charged that Roosevelt was guided by a philosophy of government that was un-American. Voters in November
were unconvinced.

The returns gave Roosevelt a sweeping victory with over 57 percent
of the popular vote and 472 of the 531 electoral votes. The numbers
are more impressive still because the majority of affiliated voters outside the South in 1932 by a large margin were traditionally Republican.
This was now to change with the formation of what came to be called
the Roosevelt coalition of urban workers, farmers, African Americans,
Catholics, Jews, and recent immigrant groups.

And so Franklin Roosevelt came to the presidency amid the nation's
greatest crisis since the Civil War. He was a disabled president determined to heal a crippled nation. He had made few detailed promises
of specific action, but inspired by his religious and political instincts,
he arrived in Washington with a determination to offer help to a struggling people. He brought with him a vision of a dynamic government
that reconciled the nationalist progressivism of Theodore Roosevelt
and Woodrow Wilson with the democratic and egalitarian ideals of
Thomas Jefferson. At the start of his presidency, he still held to some
traces of Jeffersonian suspicion of big government, albeit modified by
his government experience. These remnants, too, soon dissolved.

Before he could effectively act on long-range plans, he was forced
to deal with immediate and dangerous emergency conditions. The
nation's financial system seemed literally to be disintegrating in an
economy that had already collapsed. His inaugural warned against
fear, but fear, discouragement, and even despair troubled Americans
across the land. In his acceptance speech in Chicago, Roosevelt had
paid tribute to his countrymen for resisting the temptation to radicalism, but he acknowledged the danger.[7]

The radical temptation was real. The American press carried stories
in admiration of the efficiencies of Mussolini's regime in Italy. There
would soon be similar stories about German economic recovery under
Hitler, who came to power early in 1933. The gloom of the Depression
and distorted accounts of reform in Russia gave Communism a certain appeal to some, especially the young. Thousands joined the party
as a form of protest, a careless leap that would haunt many careers
years later during the McCarthy mania. Membership in the American
Communist party, though small, increased by 50 percent between 1929
and 1932 and then doubled by 1934 to 24,000. Various fascist groups
organized in imitation of Hitler's brown shirts. Could a wounded

capitalism and the slow-grinding wheels of democracy meet the challenges of modern times? Leading intellectuals like John Dewey, Reinhold Niebuhr, John Dos Passos, Sidney Hook, Lewis Mumford, and Lincoln Steffens concluded that capitalism was dead and turned to support more radical figures like Socialist Norman Thomas and Communist William Z. Foster. Thomas was committed to democracy, but the record reveals Communists were less fastidious about the essentials of democratic practice. Radical temptations abounded, but for the time being the electorate remained in the mainstream.

Roosevelt's mandate was clear; he had to act quickly to revive a moribund economy that seemed to have settled into a state of equilibrium at a painfully low level of productivity. There was a new danger that even this inert economy could sink deeper given the banking crisis that had been developing in the weeks before the inauguration. So began the fabled "first hundred days." In struggling to rescue an ailing capitalism and feed a hungry people, practical measures for rapid effect dominated the thought of Roosevelt and that group known as the Brain Trust that he drew to the cause.

In addition to the loyalists who had been with him for years, Howe, Rosenman, Farley, Perkins, and Hopkins, Roosevelt gathered a group of policy advisers during the campaign whom he brought into his administration in various posts and who were soon tabbed with the label "Brain Trust." The first of these was Raymond Moley, who taught political science at Columbia University. Moley eventually broke with Roosevelt, believing the New Deal went too far, and by 1936 became a Republican and increasingly conservative thereafter. Moley brought Rexford G. Tugwell and Adolph A. Berle Jr. into the group. Berle advocated reform through government and business cooperation; Tugwell was an advocate of national economic planning and became a key adviser in agricultural policy and relief of poverty. During the campaign and in the administration, the three urged greater federal activity in economic planning and in fighting the immediate effects of the Depression.

Conservatives and business interests were bankrupt of ideas beyond letting the market system play out the Depression. Congress could not trust that simple but uncertain solution and quickly ceded unprecedented powers to the new administration. Many conservative congressmen, including southern Democrats who would one day assail Roosevelt's ideas, registered no effective protests in 1933. Disorganized Republicans mounted little resistance.[8]

The collapsing banking system drew first attention from the new administration. By inauguration day, the American banking system was in acute crisis and in danger of collapse. The effects on the already suffering economy would be catastrophic. Free of any meaningful regulation or serious credit restraint from the Federal Reserve System, U.S. banks had blithely joined the army of speculators in the stock market frenzy of the 1920s. With the most relaxed concern about their borrowers' ability to repay, they loaned massive amounts to brokers and individual investors to finance their stock-picking gambles. Since the stock market seemed capable of moving in only one direction—up—and the most sober and respected financiers and economists like Bernard Baruch and Professor Irving Fisher of Yale predicted contin- ued business growth and higher securities prices, why worry? Inves- tors stretched their bets and increased their risk by using the borrowed money to buy stocks on margin with cash paying for only a small per- centage of the stock price. Banks themselves dipped into their cash reserves to buy stock, untroubled by the risk to which they were sub- jecting their unsuspecting depositors.

When the market crashed and stock values evaporated, investors, brokerage houses, and banks were embarrassingly unable to meet their obligations. In the case of the banks, those obligations were to uninsured depositors who lost their life savings (FDIC protection was a New Deal product). In the three years after the market crash, several thousand state and national banks failed. Depositor fears and rumors of more failures threatened even sound banks. As Roosevelt took office, the danger of a collapsing banking system was real.

On Sunday, March 5, the day after his inauguration, Roosevelt called Congress into emergency session and prepared a proclamation declaring a nationwide bank holiday. A whirlwind of discussions led by Raymond Moley and newly appointed Treasury Secretary William Woodin, together with cooperative Hoover administration treasury officials invited to join the sessions, produced a banking bill designed to stabilize the tottering system. On Thursday, with less than an hour of discussion, a nervous House of Representatives passed the bill; a not much more deliberative Senate followed that evening with little dissent. In the years that followed, conservatives liked to describe Roosevelt's New Deal as "socialist." The banking bill exposed the emptiness of such canards. Had Roosevelt harbored socialist sympathies, this was his opportunity. Congress was so frightened and so willing to follow his lead, he could have asked for and probably gotten legislation to nationalize the banking system. He did not ask. Before Roosevelt submitted his bill to Congress, Robert La Follette visited him to press for the establishment of a federally controlled national banking system.[9] The president declined. His aim was not to destroy capitalism but to save it. Save it he did, and a curious mix of disappointed radicals and embittered conservatives never forgave. The legislation hastily passed allowed healthy banks to reopen with government guarantees of their soundness; weaker banks were reorganized or closed. The Federal Reserve won more power to issue notes for greater capital liquidity. In June, additional legislation provided federal deposit insurance, a critical step in preventing fear-induced runs on banks.

On Sunday, March 12, the president addressed the nation in his first Fireside Chat to explain in plain language the action on the banks. With calm assurance, he convinced his audience of millions their money would be safe in the nation's banks. On Monday morning banks reopened without incident and deposits began to stream in. The crisis of the moment passed. Roosevelt's use of radio touched people as no one since (even with television) has been able to match and stimulated floods of approving mail to the White House.

During that same first week the new administration sent a farm bill to Congress. The objective was to increase the income of farmers. Because they were then still a substantial proportion of the American population, to help farm families to become consumers was an important step toward general economic recovery. The ugly irony of the Depression was a farm system that could produce bumper crops of food and fiber, which an impoverished population could not buy even at prices so low that farmers could not earn enough to pay their debts. The proposed solution was to limit production sufficiently to raise farm prices and farm income. The vehicle was the creation of the Agricultural Adjustment Administration. (AAA). The complex legislation subsidized farmers to let some land lie fallow, thus reducing production and surpluses. To the same end, the AAA also saw to the destruction of crops and animals, a stunning expedient in a hungry nation. This was not a long-term cure for farm problems, but it did allow farmers in critical economic condition to remain on their land.[10] Commodity prices and farm income did rise in the next few years, but new devices to support farm income became necessary when the Supreme Court struck down the AAA as unconstitutional in 1935.

For the industrial United States, the Hundred Days offered the National Industrial Recovery Act (NIRA), which created the National

Recovery Administration (NRA). The aim here was to do for industry what AAA was to do for farming: to help raise depressed profits of manufacturers through production codes that imposed standards and limits on producers. The NIRA also called on businesses to meet pre-scribed minimum wage and maximum hour requirements. This was designed as a cooperative effort between government, business, and labor to stimulate industrial activity and improve working conditions. Rather than subvert capitalism, FDR intended to work within and for the benefit of the system.[11] The NIRA also sought to put people to work by establishing the Public Works Administration (PWA) with an initial appropriation of over $3 billion for construction projects across the country. The Blue Eagle icon that cooperating businesses displayed became a symbol of controversy over the effectiveness of the NRA, but that argument ended when the high court also killed the NRA in 1935.

The AAA and NRA launched the American government into eco-nomic planning on a large scale. The government also assumed a role in regional planning with the establishment of the Tennessee Valley Authority (TVA) in May. Roosevelt might be described as somewhat left of center, but he did not challenge the principle of private owner-ship of the means of production on which capitalism rested. But when the opportunity presented itself for massive reclamation in the impov-erished Tennessee Valley region with the production of cheap electric power as an added benefit, he was open to an exception.

As a preparedness measure during World War I, the federal gov-ernment built dams for nitrogen-producing plants at Muscle Shoals, Tennessee, intended for producing explosives for the war effort. The operation could also produce nitrogen-based fertilizers and electric power for the region. Before the dams were completed, the war ended and the projects stalled. In the spirit of the new business-friendly con-servatism, it was decided the Muscle Shoals project should be sold to private interests. The only serious bidder for the project turned out to be Henry Ford, who offered less than five cents on the dollar that the government had already spent, and his offer was deemed acceptable. Virtually single-handedly, Senator George Norris of Nebraska blocked the sale to Ford. Norris was one of the few surviving progressives still in the Republican Party. He dreamed of a government-operated public power project that could offer low-cost fertilizers and electric power to millions of farm families in the region. He repeatedly crafted legisla-tion to turn Muscle Shoals into such a project and managed to get bills through Congress twice, but his work was killed by vetoes from Presidents Coolidge and Hoover. The big utility interests denounced Norris and called his plans socialistic. Before his inauguration, the president-elect toured the remains of the Tennessee Valley project with Norris, and, excited by the possibilities offered to one of the more depressed areas of the country, Roosevelt embraced the Norris plan.

This federally owned venture built dams on the Tennessee River in a mammoth program that put thousands to work, produced cheap electricity and fertilizers, provided for soil reclamation and conservation in a region plagued by erosion, created new recreational facilities, and served as a yardstick for the true cost of electricity production in all the areas adjoining the Tennessee Valley. The TVA was one of the most successful and enduring New Deal achievements and the only one that might be described as socialistic with some plausibility. Combined with a New Deal rural electrification program, TVA benefited a huge area of the South, many of whose representatives have ever since aimed much of their political rhetoric against the "intrusiveness" of the federal government.

In this truly amazing burst of legislative energy there was more. The Glass-Steagall Act in June prohibited speculation by banks, restrictions repealed in the last years of the 20th century with disastrous consequences. That act also established the FDIC to protect depositors and shore up confidence in banks. Attention was later addressed to strengthening confidence in the honesty of securities trading. In June, the Securities Act was passed to require more candid disclosure of details concerning new stock issues. Later, in June 1934, the Congress established the Securities and Exchange Commission to check irresponsible actions of market manipulators. Roosevelt appointed Joseph P. Kennedy to head the commission. Kennedy had been fabulously successful in the market, anticipated the decline, and husbanded his gains before the crash. Some of those profits he contributed to Roosevelt's 1932 campaign. It was a shrewd appointment of a man who understood the market, knew the traders, and understood their manipulations of the system. Against Wall Street resistance, Kennedy successfully ushered through new regulations and set up effective commission oversight. After decades of effective operation, flaccid enforcement allowed regulations established during the New Deal to be breached with ease in the first decade of this century, again with painful results.

With this array of new laws Roosevelt was building on the work of Theodore Roosevelt and Woodrow Wilson in establishing an American response to the realities of modern industrial and finance capitalism. While the rest of the industrialized world experimented with Marxist and fascist solutions to modern economic production, he was the architect of a system of federally regulated capitalism to harness some of its power and to check its worst acquisitive excesses. The unfettered free market system, embraced with near religious fervor by business classes and academic economists up to that time, seemed to be programmed to generate periods of prosperity followed regularly by collapses exacting excruciating human costs. Roosevelt tried to preserve the healthy incentives of market capitalism while introducing rational policing of abuses and moderating the more pernicious effects of the business cycle through government planning and oversight. The regulatory structure born of the New Deal established a new American capitalism. The nation has argued ever since about whether there has been too much regulation or not enough, and the conservative consensus of the late 20th century ached to dismantle the structure, but it has so far remained largely in place despite some erosion and worrisome neglect of effective oversight.

In 1933 something more was desperately needed besides regulatory controls. Beneficent results from the structural changes would take time; meanwhile people were hungry. Nothing before or since in the national experience of Americans approached the breadth and intensity of want in the United States. If farmers had not been hit badly enough by economic conditions, nature added more pain. Several years of drought conditions struck so severely that crops withered and unmeasured tons of powder-dry topsoil blew away. Agrarians had been abandoning farm life for decades, moving to the cities to find work. Now escape to the cities confronted them with armies of the urban unemployed also looking for jobs. By 1933, unemployment in the United States reached 25 percent, and many of those with jobs worked only part-time. Wages had fallen to near ten cents an hour in many industries. From 1930 to 1932, 600,000 homeowners lost their property. Breadlines, soup kitchens, and homeless families living in makeshift shelters in "Hoovervilles" became part of American cityscapes. Aside from the systemic restructuring, something had to be done to deliver quick aid to the masses of American poor until recovery lifted the economy. So another stream of the Hundred Days of legislation focused on immediate humanitarian help.[12]

Late in March, Roosevelt asked for and in April Congress passed legislation establishing the Federal Emergency Relief Administration

(FERA). One-half billion dollars was appropriated and the president named Harry Hopkins, who had administered relief programs for Roosevelt in New York, as its administrator. As head of FERA, Hopkins struggled to provide immediate relief to the needy without contributing to a demoralizing dependency.[13]

Just days after taking office, FDR proposed a scheme to combine unemployment relief with the conservation of natural resources. By the end of March, Congress approved the creation of the Civilian Conservation Corps (CCC). The object was to get idle young men off the desperate streets and into productive work conserving natural resources. The CCC was one of the most popular New Deal programs, and for Roosevelt, a longtime champion of reforestation and conservation, one of his favorites. It was also one of the most successful of his initiatives, astonishingly so in the speed with which it delivered benefits, economic and natural. Those were multiple. Approved on March 31, 1,300 CCC camps were open by mid-June, and by the end of July over 300,000 young men were working in the woodlands. Like much of the New Deal, it was an experimental and practical response to a crisis condition; it met an important human need, and it improved the nation's natural resources. Millions of trees were planted, firebreaks cut, soil erosion checked, underbrush cleared, and parks built. Over its life, the CCC benefitted the health and education of over 3 million young men, who sent, as required, a substantial portion of their modest earnings to their families back home. It was a program that cut across racial lines, although pressure was required to convince southern officials to recruit young black men for the Corps. In the end, about 10 percent of CCC men were black. Decades later, old men recalled positive and grateful memories of CCC service.[14]

The flood of legislation, effective communication, the reassuring confidence of the president, and his obvious concern for a suffering people informed a Washington atmosphere in sharp contrast to the days of Herbert Hoover. But nothing so sharply dramatized the difference between the two administrations as their response to veterans marching to and camping in the capital city to protest their perceived neglect. The Bonus Army of thousands of veterans marched to Washington in the summer of 1932 to insist on accelerated payment of promised bonuses for service in the World War. They encamped at Anacostia Flats, hoping to spur government action. Hoover refused any contact with the veterans. Congress failed to move on a bonus bill, but the veterans, many with their families, refused to leave in protest and in the hope that Congress might yet act. On July 28, when police were ordered to clear away some veteran squatters on Pennsylvania Avenue, they responded to rock throwing by firing on the veterans with live ammunition. At that point, the White House ordered army troops to help the police. A steed-mounted Douglas MacArthur, exceeding Hoover's intent, led a stunning force of infantry accompanied by machine-gun units and several tanks, against the veterans. MacArthur denounced the assembly as a revolution in the making. The veterans and their families were routed and their protest ended.

In May 1933, another corps of veterans several thousand strong went to Washington to renew their demands. Roosevelt ordered bedding and food prepared, medics provided basic care, a military band played daily. Mrs. Roosevelt paid a visit to their encampment, brought the president's greetings, and listened to their stories. "Before she left the camp, she joined in a chorus of a bittersweet song brought back from the war: 'There's a long trail a-winding, to the land of my dreams. . . .' They sent her off with cheers."[15] Camp leaders were brought to the White House to meet and talk with the president. Although their demands could not be met, Roosevelt invited the veterans to join the CCC and suspended the age limits for entry into the Corps. By the hundreds, they joined, and others were supplied with train fare home.

The Hundred Days was an amazing period of improvisation. FDR did not come to the presidency with a detailed plan, but he came with an instinct. He knew the depth of the nation's problems, and he knew that orthodox economic and political responses were not working. So he improvised remedies, confronting each piece of the collage of problems with an experimental solution. Democracy in crisis was not condemned to paralysis but inspired to action unrestrained by the chains of past certitudes. The Hundred Days constituted part of what is labeled the First New Deal, which turned away from the idea that competition in a free market economy would bring timely recovery. Unconvinced that the economy would right itself, the First New Deal generated an immediate humanitarian response to help a suffering people and fast action to stimulate economic recovery so that a people returning to productive work could help themselves. Roosevelt's early political, ethical, and religious convictions, sharpened and tempered by the experience of digging out of the crisis of 1933, profoundly influenced the Second New Deal launched in 1935. That effort was to seek a long-term prescription for national well-being—a new social contract. This was the path to the Roosevelt revolution.

6

The Third Revolution—Phase II

The outpouring of legislation to fight the Depression during 1933 and 1934 was stunning. Economic progress was stubbornly slow, but hope revived. Millions benefited from relief and from work that was generated as the country's infrastructure was recast and its landscape renewed. No administration had ever squeezed as much from a Congress now moved both by fearful conditions and inspired leadership. Banking legislation, NRA, AAA, TVA, CCC, FERA, FHA to insure mortgage loans; the litany went on. Five hundred million dollars was provided in loans for low-cost housing. When Harold Ickes moved too cautiously in approving projects under the Public Works Administration, Roosevelt established the Civil Works Administration (CWA) with the help of the smoothly efficient Harry Hopkins, and a flood of federal money financed thousands of projects ranging from laying sewer pipe and new construction to hiring in recreation, education, and the arts. A grateful nation was impressed and rewarded the president with even more Democrats elected to Congress in the mid-term elections.

What is often described as the Second New Deal began in 1935. The objective was ". . . somehow or other to give the plain people a better break in a darkly confusing world."[1] It was the core of the Roosevelt revolution because with it he worked permanent changes in American life. Here was long-term reform to be achieved by forcing basic elements of a welfare state on a more than reluctant capitalist establishment. The Second New Deal was a product of philosophical conviction, and it was a response to the stubborn resistance to change by the capitalists and the courts. As the prospects of cooperative action with the business community dimmed, Roosevelt opted for mandated social and economic restructure. As business hostility grew, so did assaults by the courts. The great challenge came in May 1935, when the Supreme Court, in *Schechter v. U.S.*, struck down the NRA as unconstitutional, threatening the survival of much of the rest of New Deal legislation.

Roosevelt was already thinking of his new agenda when the urging of his more progressive advisors and the threat of judicial obstruction toughened his resolve. Action began early in the year and in June, after the Schechter decision, he called in Democratic congressional leaders and pressed for action on a full program of new reforms. Fighting Depression conditions remained high on the administration agenda. Unemployment remained mercilessly high with its consequent hardships. In April Roosevelt signed the Emergency Relief Administration Act, which gave the president extraordinary powers to spend at his discretion almost $5 billion in new work projects—an astonishing sum for its day. The legislation outraged conservatives and worried even leaders of organized labor, concerned about what they thought would be a depressing effect on the wages of those who had jobs. By executive order he created the Works Progress Administration (WPA). Roosevelt, always troubled by a simple relief dole, was much more comfortable when aid was combined with the dignity of work. Over the life of the program, the WPA put more than 8 million people to work and spent $11 billion. Through the WPA, FDR's humanitarianism produced economic, social, and cultural rehabilitation. Over 21,000 projects to construct or repair schools, airports, roads, hospitals, courthouses, and public parks were completed across the country. Projects for artists, writers, and actors employed thousands and offered instruction, beauty, and entertainment to millions. Few acts of government were as immediately beneficent to individuals and to society.[2]

Again, Roosevelt assigned a key task to Harry Hopkins, who performed brilliantly as usual. After Louis Howe, Hopkins developed a closer relationship to FDR and to Eleanor Roosevelt than any of the other White House advisors. Indeed, in his last years, Hopkins, as Howe had, lived in the White House. Sharply intelligent, steadfastly devoted to the cause of social reform for a lifetime, his views were often identical with Eleanor's and sometimes ahead of the president. His relationship with the president, solid from the start, grew so strong with time as to make him indispensable. Roosevelt tapped him for advice and trouble-shooting on a wide range of issues in domestic and even in foreign affairs. Having abandoned an interest in socialism, which he had entertained in his youth, Hopkins was convinced that the survival of capitalism depended on its changing and adapting to modern circumstances, a view long held by his boss. The necessary changes would have to come, he thought, through government intervention. He pressed for the kind of federal action that unfolded in the New Deal and looked for action in areas the New Deal was not able to go, including national health insurance, housing, and education.[3] Eventually, the GI Bill of Rights made a start at government help in housing and education; health insurance would have to wait. Roosevelt relied on no one during his presidency more often and with greater confidence than Harry Hopkins.

Although he came to be revered by the working class, Roosevelt's relations with organized labor were not always smooth. He was disappointed when AFL leaders expressed fears that CCC wages of a dollar a day would depress wages generally.[4] Much of his administration's work was aimed at improving the conditions of workers, but he did not come into office as a champion of organized labor, and there was little direct legislation in the first years to encourage unionization. Roosevelt did not take part in shaping the National Labor Relations Act. That was the child of Senator Robert Wagner, Democrat of New York. Wagner and Roosevelt were allies in the New York Assembly years earlier. Wagner's political career was consistently committed to improving the working conditions of the industrial laboring classes. Elected to the U. S. Senate in 1926, he drafted reform laws that withered in the arid conditions of the decade of normalcy. With the coming of the New Deal, Wagner made his mark. He contributed to drafting a long list of legislation including the NIRA, FERA, CCC, and especially the National Labor Relations Act, which bears his name as the Wagner Act.

The president's first reaction to Wagner's draft was marked by concern that the act would encourage labor strife and retard recovery. As a progressive, and as governor and president, Roosevelt had long supported improving the condition of the laboring classes, but he had not been an outspoken champion of unions, as had Wagner, who saw strong unions as the vehicle for increasing worker income. The resulting increase in consumption would also be economically stimulating. The senator was a member of the National Labor Board under the NRA but grew increasingly frustrated by business resistance and the board's weak powers. In March 1934, he introduced legislation to increase the board's authority, but could not win administration support. He tried again in February 1935, with an even stronger bill.

The bill passed the Senate by an overwhelming vote of 63 to 12 in May 1935, and before House action was completed, a nimble Roosevelt embraced the legislation as essential and threw his support behind it. When challenged he denied that unions would become too powerful. Rather, he saw unions as a democratic counterforce to business power. The law created a new National Labor Relations Board to oversee election of collective bargaining units, check unfair labor practices by business, and protect the right of workers to organize. For generations government had usually been indifferent or hostile to the cause of labor. Fearful insecurity plagued workers daring enough to work toward or even talk about unionization. Summary dismissals, blackballing, yellow-dog contracts, scab labor, and violence were the standard weapons of corporations defying worker efforts to organize. The Wagner Act placed the authority of the government behind the right of workers to organize and bargain collectively. It proved a boon to unionization and marked an important turning point in the history of organized labor in the United States. The fabulous growth of capitalist enterprise in the United States as unions multiplied and grew stronger belied the earnest predictions of the business community that unions would bring economic doom.[5]

In June 1935, Roosevelt sent a message to Congress calling for revision of the tax code, a measure that won him the undying opprobrium of the luxuriously and even the modestly wealthy. The power to tax, it was famously said, is the power to destroy. The power to tax also carries with it the power to restructure income distribution and economic influence in more just proportions. This was the president's stated purpose. "Our revenue laws have operated in many ways to the unfair advantage of the few, and they have done little to prevent the unjust concentration of wealth and economic power." He proposed a tax on "inherited economic power" and the upward revision of graduated rates on the incomes of the very rich. It was equitable, he said, "to adjust our tax system in accordance with economic capacity, advantage and fact."[6]

The most enduring and defining action of the Roosevelt revolution was the creation of the social security system. He himself saw the Social Security Act as central to his whole program and the proudest achievement of his domestic administration.[7] Nothing better served as emblematic of the New Deal than this legislation. Here was the real basis of a modern welfare state. When FDR created the Committee on Economic Security in June 1934, he asked Secretary of Labor Frances Perkins to lead it in producing a program of social insurance. It was not a novel idea. Creating a minimal standard of security against improvidence in an industrial society wherein age, accident, or economic chance could dissolve wages reached back many years. Socialists were the early advocates; a conservative German government enacted a pension system in the late 19th century; papal encyclicals supported the idea as a matter of justice. Theodore Roosevelt included the idea in the 1912 Progressive platform; Franklin Roosevelt spoke of it as governor of New York. A few states enacted old-age insurance laws, but they reached few people and were badly underfunded. FDR wanted a program based on the insurance model that would require contributions for the recipients and would be self-supporting.[8] Some of his advisers, including Perkins and Rexford Tugwell argued that payroll contributions would be a regressive tax on workers, but a cunning Roosevelt insisted. "We put those payroll contributions there so as to give the contributors a legal, moral, and political right to collect their pensions and their unemployment benefits. With those taxes in there, no damn politician can ever scrap my social security program."[9] It was not an idle fear; some "damn politicians" have indeed sought such a scrapping in the name of free market liberties, but without success thus far.

In his annual message to Congress in January 1935, the president alerted the legislature that he would ask for action to provide "security against the major hazards of life" and argued that a survey showing that many countries had successfully done so proved it was time for the United States to act.[10] Days later, he sent the legislation to the Hill. The bill provided for old-age pensions; federal aid to the needy, aged, the blind, and orphaned children; aid to the disabled; and federally supervised, but state-administered, unemployment compensation. The act did not cover everyone and payroll deduction was a regressive feature, but whatever its faults, it provided a historic turn of great consequence. It assigned social responsibility for the needy to the whole community through its government, and it recognized the social rights of citizens. The Constitution invested the federal government with responsibility for the "general welfare"; here was a new departure in fulfilling that responsibility. Over the decades the Social Security Administration has served millions dependably, with great efficiency, and at overhead costs dramatically lower than those of private insurance.

The House of Representatives passed the Social Security Act in April by an overwhelming vote of 371–33. The Senate followed in June by a vote of 76 to 6, and the president signed the law on August 15. The House vote does not reflect the fact that all but one Republican voted for a procedural maneuver to block passage of the bill that they claimed would result in calamity. In the Senate, 12 of 19 Republicans supported a failed effort to eliminate the old-age pension provisions.

Conservatives generally were appalled, and they responded with a venom that could not be restrained. One congressman announced: "The lash of the dictator will be felt. And twenty-million free American citizens will for the first time submit themselves to a fingerprint test." Said another, "Never in the history of the world has any measure been brought in here so insidiously designed as to prevent business recovery, to enslave workers, and to prevent any possibility of the employers providing work for the people."[11] Businessmen like Alfred Sloan, the head of General Motors, foresaw an end to capitalist virtues, and the National Association of Manufacturers issued a statement warning of the emergent socialism. Conservatives charged that the law abandoned traditional American self-reliance and promised moral decay. The survival of the republic itself was threatened. Some southerners feared the law would destroy the incentive to work among blacks. During the 1936 presidential campaign, Republican candidate Alf Landon called the law unjust and unworkable, a cruel hoax on working men. The Republican National Committee prepared materials for posters and payroll envelopes suggesting to workers that they would be suffering a pay cut through the payroll deductions, but making no mention of benefits.[12]

The fear mongering was futile. The social security programs were popular from the start and worked very well in fulfilling the intention of the legislation to establish a minimal security against privation. In a 1940 speech Roosevelt spoke of the obligation of the government to provide a minimum old-age pension for *every* needy man or woman in the country. In succeeding decades coverage was extended to more people—including the self-employed—benefits improved, and in 1966 Congress added Medicare provisions for the elderly to the system in what many hoped would be a step toward universal health care. Conservatives have never entirely abandoned their discomfort with the social security system, but many decades of its operation have produced no evidence that social security causes moral decay; the republic still lives.[13]

Despite conservative reservations, few actions of the United States government have been as broadly supported as the social security system. Here was the heart of the Roosevelt revolution. Here was the communal commitment to economic well-being. The American electorate registered its approval in the election of 1936. The Republicans nominated Alf Landon, governor of Kansas, a man of progressive Republican roots. Despite conservative domination of the party, Landon was the first of a series of nominees from the more moderate side of the party including Wendell Willkie in 1940, Thomas Dewey in 1944 and 1948, and Dwight Eisenhower in 1952. Landon presented a great contrast to Roosevelt in style and personality. He was not a very effective speaker, and although he had approved some early New Deal measures, he was saddled with the nation's memories of the Hoover years and his party's bitter hostility to the New Deal.

During the campaign, Roosevelt focused on the unfinished work still to be done and on the resistance to change from conservative anti-New Deal forces. Accepting re-nomination at the Democratic Convention in Philadelphia, the president pointed to the undemocratic concentration of power in the hands of the moneyed with a phrase that stuck as a label for his enemies and a memorable moment among years of presidential speeches. "These economic royalists complain that we seek to overthrow the institutions of America. What they really complain of is that we seek to take away their power." They are willing enough for government to assure a citizen's right to vote, but not for government to "do anything to protect the citizen in his right to work and his right to live." Deflecting charges that his administration was radical, even Communist, he opened that election campaign in September with the claim that the New Deal had saved the country from radicals like the Communists who fed on the economic hard times. Liberalism had performed a conserving function. Paraphrasing Thomas Babington Macaulay, he exhorted, "Reform if you would preserve." And he concluded, "I am that kind of conservative because I am that kind of liberal." Closing his campaign at Madison Square Garden, he continued to hammer at his business critics. His administration had to struggle against the monopolists, the reckless bankers, and the speculators, who regarded the government merely as servants of their own interests. "And we know now that Government by organized money is just as dangerous as government by organized mob." The crowd cheered wildly.[14]

As usual Roosevelt enjoyed campaigning, drawing sustenance from the cheering crowds. This was important in 1936 given the increasingly bitter and personal quality of the attacks on him. He was well aware now that cooperation across class lines was not going to happen. But this could not seriously dampen the confidence with which he returned to Hyde Park for voting and the election returns. Newspaper editorials and the infamous *Literary Digest* poll predicting a Landon victory aside, the signs pointed to a comfortable victory, even a landslide. That benighted journal made its confident prediction having polled a list of telephone subscribers and owners of automobiles, hardly a representative sampling of the American electorate in mid-Depression. Despite continuing hard times, the record of the New Deal held broad appeal. Since 1932, unemployment numbers were down by 4 million; 6 million new jobs had been created; manufacturing payrolls doubled, stock prices doubled; farm incomes were dramatically higher, and industrial production had almost doubled.[15] The visible action of a caring government and the sense of trust in Roosevelt solidified the support of the electorate behind the president and deflected the impact of the vociferous but ultimately inept challengers. The bland Landon could not bring a moribund Republican party to life. Al Smith, who could never quite adjust to Roosevelt's displacing him, spoke for the Liberty League of well-to-do conservatives, but they themselves were his only audience. Demagogic characters like Huey Long (killed in 1935), Gerald L. K. Smith, and Father Charles Coughlin helped to organize a third-party movement in the hope of drawing votes away from Roosevelt. The Union party nominated William Lemke of North Dakota with little effect on the vote.

If the election of 1936 was a referendum on Roosevelt's performance, the people registered their judgment with great clarity. The result was one of the great landslides of American electoral history with Roosevelt winning more than 60 percent of the popular vote. His electoral majority was 523 to 8. Roosevelt's coattails and popular disgust with the Republicans brought overwhelming Democratic majorities to Congress, 331 to 89 in the House and 76 of the 96 seats in the Senate. There were so many Democrats in the Senate chamber that some had to be seated across the aisle on the traditionally Republican side. The nation approved; the mandate was his, but despite the triumph, frustration and disappointment lay ahead.

By 1935 an unfriendly Supreme Court threatened to undermine much of the New Deal, having overturned key provisions of the NRA and AAA. How would new initiatives be treated by the Court? Would every effort at recovery and reform encounter narrowly rigid constitutional interpretations in defense of extreme readings of contract and property rights? This was particularly bitter given the overwhelming mandate voters had given the New Deal in the elections of 1934 and the landslide of 1936. Six of the nine justices were over 70 and had been trained in the law in the heyday of the great corporate giants when their skilled lawyers and friendly courts shaped their reading of the Constitution in stalwart defense of corporate property interests. Now they continued to apply the strongest defenses against regulatory intervention by government. The presumed danger led Roosevelt to his most controversial and costly move in domestic politics, and judged by many commentators as his most serious mistake.

In February 1937, Roosevelt presented his court "reform" legislation to the Congress. The plan provided that the president be allowed to appoint one additional justice to the nine-member Supreme Court for every justice who did not retire upon reaching age 70 and six months, up to a total of six additions. The thinly veiled and unconvincing cover story argued that this plan would help the overburdened court get its work done with more dispatch. In the reigning circumstances, the president would have been able add six new justices to the Court and recolor the complexion of its decisions. A great furor erupted. For conservatives the plan confirmed all the worst misgivings about Roosevelt. Among the unconvinced, including even many liberals, the president lost much support for what was seen as "court packing" and a challenge to the principle of separation of powers. The plan did much damage before a change of heart in the Court and the quiet death of the Court reform bill in committee ended the crisis.

Among the reasons that prompted Roosevelt to act were the decisions of the Court, by 5 to 4 margins, to strike down state minimum wage laws, this at a time when the administration was working on social security, unemployment insurance, and its own national minimum wage proposal. Thus the apprehension. The roadblock cleared in March, however, when one of the conservative majority, Justice Owen Roberts, switched sides and voted to uphold a Washington state minimum wage law almost identical to one from New York that the Court had rejected in 1935. Roosevelt lost the court battle, and with it the allegiance of some independent and even some liberal supporters that he would not regain. But perhaps he won the war. His plan for the court may, indeed, have stimulated a change of judicial heart and broken through the wall of resistance to reform legislation. The Court next rendered a positive decision on the Wagner Act. The resignation of three justices followed over the period of a year, and new appointees worked a sharp change in the Court's view of constitutional restraints.

The Court battle was painful and damaging to the administration, but the switch of interpretation on the minimum wage cleared the way for another key initiative of the Roosevelt revolution. Late in May 1937, with constitutional barriers apparently razed, Roosevelt sent to the Congress legislation on wages and hours. He told the Congress, "A self-supporting and self-respecting democracy can plead no justification for the existence of child labor, no economic reason for chiseling workers' wages or stretching workers' hours."[16] Industry critics performed as scripted, warning that a minimum wage would spark competition from imports produced at lower labor costs. Leaders of organized labor, always slower in support of Roosevelt than the rank and file, expressed fears that the minimum would be regarded as a maximum wage and weaken collective bargaining. After Congress adjourned in Washington's August heat, Roosevelt called a special session for November 15. Roosevelt understood what businessmen had consistently resisted in the 1920s and remained slow to see even in the Depression: raising the income of the working class was not only just and humane, it was economically sound. "What does the country ultimately gain if we encourage business men to enlarge the capacity of American industry to produce, unless we see to it that the income of our working population actually expands sufficiently to create markets to absorb that increased production?"[17]

Judicial roadblocks were removed, but now the political machinery stalled the drive for minimum wage legislation. The court fight cost the president some support in Congress and added more cohesion to the emerging alliance between Republicans and increasingly conservative southern Democrats, both firmly resistant to federal power encroaching on states' prerogatives. That wages were lower in the southern industries was not seen as a disadvantage to the region by many of its representatives. There was, as well, a curious alliance between these conservative forces and key leaders of organized labor, when William Green, president of the American Federation of Labor, opposed the legislation.[18] Procedural maneuvers blocked action in the special session, and in January, Roosevelt told the new session that the American people overwhelmingly supported wage legislation.

He tried to reassure labor: "We are seeking, of course, only legislation to end starvation wages and intolerable hours; more desirable wages are and should continue to be a product of collective bargaining."[19] After more infighting and legislative snarls, a Wage and Hour Act was approved by Congress in June. With some industries exempted, the law established a minimum wage of 25 cents an hour to be raised gradually to 40 cents, and a 44-hour work week to be gradually reduced to 40 hours. It was a long struggle to reach a level of minimum decency. With a prejudice that Harry Truman once sarcastically described as "the lower the minimum the better the wage," business interests argued then and ever since that raising minimum wages would discourage hiring, cost existing jobs, and reduce productivity. That these results never materialized has not discouraged repetition of the argument.

Wage and hour legislation was another piece of the Roosevelt revolution that changed lives as it became a permanent feature of the economic landscape. It defied the Ricardian market theory that subsistence wages were inevitable, and it added another role for government to play against the exploitation of those with the weakest leverage in the labor market place.

The hard struggle and tortuous process that plagued the wage and hour law was one of several signs of growing resistance to New Deal programs. As noted, the court fight angered even some of FDR's liberal supporters. Because it was a one-party South, Democrats from the region made up a large portion of the Democratic majorities in the House and Senate. Those Democratic majorities were large but somewhat misleading because Democrats from the South often sided with the Republicans, especially after 1937. An exception and strong Roosevelt ally, Senator Claude Pepper of Florida, angrily railed at the conservative coalition that had grown to oppose and frustrate late New Deal measures. He accused its partisans of hating Roosevelt and sabotaging efforts to help American workers. They catered, he charged, to a "handful of Wall Street speculators" and "international money changers who have no flag and no cause but money." Among the southerners he probably had in mind were Democrats like Carter Glass and Harry Bird of Virginia, Millard Tydings of Maryland, and especially Thomas P. Gore of Oklahoma, who spoke much like a social Darwinist.[20]

For several years, Roosevelt, without being fully persuaded, had ceded to economic advisors and Depression necessity in adopting what came to be known as Keynesian economic measures. John Maynard Keynes was a British economist from Cambridge University who earned a great reputation in the profession and beyond with his book, *The Economic Consequences of the Peace*, in 1919. In that work, he predicted economic disaster because of the exorbitant reparations payments imposed on a defeated Germany. His most important work was *The General Theory of Employment, Interest, and Money*, published in 1936, which gathered the ideas for which he was already powerfully influential among a new generation of young economists. His ideas represented a sharp break with the traditional "classical" economics, which had dominated the business world and university instruction. He broke with the cherished ideas about the importance of balanced government budgets and the fixed rule that market declines, even depressions, are in the long run self correcting. Keynes' famous rejoinder asserted, "In the long run we are all dead." He expressed the fear, which appeared to carry weight in the 1930s, that collapsed economies could establish long-term equilibrium at a stagnant bottom. The core of his revolution in economic thought lay in the notion that in a recession or depression the crucial problem was a lack of circulating money. Since a stagnant economy had great difficulty stimulating itself, it behooved government to act. Here was the counter-intuitive element: the prescription required that government increase spending and lower taxes during hard times, balanced budget be damned, in order to put people back to work, simulate economic activity, and reverse the downward spiral of prices, wages, and profits. A recovered economy would eventually produce sufficient revenues to pay off the government debt and return its budget to balance.

Roosevelt was somewhat traditional in his economic views and was not as entirely convinced by or comfortable with these new ideas as some of his aides. His 1932 campaign had sincerely held out the hope of a balanced budget, and the great deficits of his first years in office were generated by the emergency and humanitarian demands of a suffering people. When the economic indicators finally showed some strength in the right direction, Roosevelt mistook the measurable improvement in 1936 as a signal that he could return to what was for him the more comfortable common sense idea that budgets ought to be balanced. This he tried with an immediately resulting rise in unemployment and a new recession in 1937. It is often repeated with only casual attention to accuracy that the New Deal failed to end the Great Depression, whose malaise was cured only by the massive spending for World War II. It is a distortion that resists amendment. In April 1938, Roosevelt, returning to Keynesian ideas, summoned a special session of Congress, which passed a massive new spending measure appropriating over $5 billion for public works and economic pump-priming. Within months the economy responded in tune with Keynesian predictions. Depression hardship was not over, but by late 1939, before the huge expenditures for war materials added their own stimulus, the signs of recovery were clear enough in the key economic indicators. Production rose by over 25 percent from May 1937 to August 1939; 2 million new jobs were added; steel production more than doubled; and the unemployment rate fell below 8 percent. It is not unreasonable to conclude that the economy was on a path to full recovery *before* the massive war expenditures took effect.[21]

Reform energies, especially after the hurricane of changes since 1933, were difficult to sustain in a more reluctant Congress after 1938. Thus the wage and hour bill was among the last of the New Deal reform measures passed, and the attentions of the Congress and the president were drawn more and more to world affairs and then war. There was, however, one more chapter of the revolution to be written. That concerned a Roosevelt initiative that proved irresistible to even the most hard-shelled conservatives. It was the GI Bill of Rights. When he signed a military draft law covering young men 18 and 19 years old in November 1942, Roosevelt appointed a committee of educators to study the matter of the interrupted education of those who served. This was a clue to his thinking about the lives of veterans after the war. In October 1943, he proposed to Congress legislation to make good the nation's obligation to those who fought to defend it. Education—vocational, general, and professional—was the key to the future well-being of veterans and important for the country as well. War service interrupted the acquisition of the knowledge and skills the young would need to earn a productive living. "We must replenish our supply of persons qualified to discharge the heavy responsibilities of the post-war world. We have taught our youth how to wage war; we must also teach them how to live useful and happy lives in freedom, justice and liberty."[22] He urged support not only for direct costs of education but for maintenance while in school as well.

Both logic and emotion drove the legislation through both houses of a Congress, now generally unfriendly to New Deal ideas, by unanimous votes, and the president signed the Servicemen's Readjustment Act, the GI Bill of Rights, in June 1944. This last step of the Roosevelt revolution crucially eased the transition of millions from war production to a peacetime economy and radically reshaped the American nation. The law provided for education and training for up to a total of four years with money for books, tuition, and living expenses. Unmarried veterans received stipends of $65 per month; those with one or more dependents received $90. The law also guaranteed loans for the purchase of homes and for business starts. Over 2 million loan guarantees were delivered by 1950. For those searching for immediate entry into the job market, unemployment compensation of $20 a week was available for 52 weeks.

The results were spectacular. Young people for whom cost or family obligations had put college education out of reach in the past now flooded the classrooms. By early in 1948 almost 2 million veterans attended schools of various kinds; over a half million received job training; and veterans made up almost half of all college enrollments. What was once the realm of privilege was now open to the masses. For millions of the children of those veterans higher education was to be normal rather than exceptional. The benefit to the nation in skills and productivity was immeasurable. Roosevelt understood that the standards set by the G I Bill would serve all citizens after the war as a Second Bill of Rights to which he had referred in his annual address to Congress in January 1944.[23]

When Harry Truman inherited the presidency in April 1945, the United States was a very different country than it had been when a dour Herbert Hoover accompanied Franklin Roosevelt to his inauguration in March 1933. Looking out on the world, the United States was a new superpower. At home the basics remained. Democracy and capitalism informed the American experience, but both had been altered. Government by the people now assumed a greater fraternal responsibility to provide for the general welfare of the people. As with the achievement of a more perfect liberty and equality, more had to be done, and the Roosevelt revolution pointed the way.

Counterrevolutionaries

Franklin Roosevelt was a beloved figure to millions of Americans who responded to his warmth, to the hope he inspired, and to the political and social revolution he led. But he was also reviled at several points on the political spectrum, by the elite classes whose position of exclusive privilege he challenged, by disappointed radicals, and by demagogues of eccentric vision who craved power. One well-to-do hater thought that only Roosevelt's death would save the country from ruin, and another announced that he wanted to hear no news until he had heard that FDR had died. A Connecticut country club adopted a rule barring the mention of the president's name in the club to avoid "a health menace" for its members. On the other hand, American Communist leader Earl Browder accused Roosevelt of leading a capitalist attack on the people.[1] Radicals saw the New Deal as tragic because its reforms undermined the appeal of radicalism. Norman Thomas, presidential candidate of the Socialist Party, said: "What cut the ground out pretty completely from under us . . . was Roosevelt in a word. You don't need anything more."[2]

The president's most severe and in some ways most politically dangerous critics were not the Communists or the more moderate Socialist Party of Thomas, but individual demagogues who drew to themselves large popular followings. Had Roosevelt not succeeded in alleviating the worst of the Depression suffering and invested the country with a sense of movement and hope, potential for great turmoil and trouble lay in the hands of men like Huey Long, Gerald L. K. Smith, Francis Townsend, and Charles Coughlin.

Huey Long was the flamboyant governor of Louisiana whose populist rhetoric and policies drew a large following in the 1920s. He remained the virtual boss of the state even after his election to the U. S. Senate in 1931. He carried his populist ideas to Washington with inflammatory orations assaulting evil bankers and the powerful super-wealthy who had brought such suffering to the people. Long supported FDR in the election of 1932 but soon broke with the administration because it would not go far enough in redistributing the wealth of the nation. In 1934 he proclaimed his "Share Our Wealth" program, one feature of which was a 100 percent tax on incomes over $1 million. With the money so gathered, he promised a guaranteed income to every family in the United States, free education through college level, old-age pensions, and other largesse. Details on how all this would be accomplished were meager. Looking toward 1936, he joined with Smith and Coughlin in plans to form a third party. Long did not intend to be a candidate in 1936. The strategy, according to his biographer, T. Harry Williams, was to draw enough votes from Roosevelt to cause his defeat. A Republican administration would cause more hardship, and the way would be clear for Long to rescue the country by election to the presidency in 1940.[3] Fate dictated differently when a gunman assassinated Long in the capitol building in Baton Rouge in September 1935.

Gerald L. K. Smith became a spokesman and organizer for Long's "Share Our Wealth" scheme, establishing clubs around the country dedicated to the plan. Smith, too, was given to strident, fiery speeches. He called Eleanor Roosevelt a "female Rasputin" and referred to the president as a "communist, and atheist and a cripple." After Long's assassination he convinced many of Long's followers to join Townsend and Coughlin in forming the Union Party for the election of 1936. During the campaign, his claims and accusations were so wild that Townsend and Union presidential candidate William Lemke disowned him.[4] After extravagantly high expectations, Smith was bitterly disappointed by the paltry performance of the party in the election. He did, however, continue a career of stoking extremism, advocating isolationism, touting white supremacy, and preaching virulent racism and anti-Semitism.

Until their falling out, Smith, Francis E. Townsend, and Charles Coughlin partnered in vitriolic attacks on Roosevelt and in support of the third party candidacy of Lemke. Townsend was an elderly California physician, 67 years old in 1934, who promoted a plan to end the hard times. The Townsend Plan proposed that every citizen aged 60 and older be sent a pension of $200 per month with the condition that the money would be spent within 30 days. The elderly would be solvent and the money would circulate immediately into the economy. The cost was to be met with a national sales tax. In August 1934, he began a petition drive in support of the idea, and this was soon transformed into a successful movement to establish Townsend clubs across the country. That the plan was not economically sound did not diminish its popular appeal or its political potential. Townsend's anti-Roosevelt passion led him to advise supporters to vote for Landon in states where Lemke's name was not on the presidential ballot. Association with third-party extremism and the advent of the Roosevelt's social security system relegated the Townsend Plan to a background story.

Charles Coughlin was the "radio priest" who drew a huge national audience to his broadcasts from Royal Oak, Michigan. Like Long, he was at first a supporter of Roosevelt and the New Deal. Early on he declared it was Roosevelt or ruin for the country. He attacked ungodly capitalism with increasing venom, but eventually turned his violent ranting against the president, whom he charged with coddling the bankers and with being insufficiently radical. Coughlin spewed condemnations in all directions, damning communism, fascism, socialism, and capitalism. He did not, however, offer any coherent alternative except that Christian social justice should be engineered through powerful government controls. That prescription did not restrain him from condemning what he regarded as the excessive bureaucracy of the New Deal. He joined the Union Party effort to unseat Roosevelt, and described the president as a man surrounded by atheists and communists. After the humiliating showing of the Union Party, Coughlin redoubled his slashing attacks against Roosevelt, Bolshevism, the "conspiracy of Jewish bankers," and other assorted evils. These were accompanied by friendly comments about the accomplishments of the governments of Hitler and Mussolini. Coughlin reached an enormous audience, and, as a priest, had a special appeal for some Catholics. Many, including Catholics, were appalled. A leading Catholic social reformer and respected critic of abusive capitalism, Monsignor John Ryan, spoke out against Coughlin and rallied to the support of Roosevelt in 1936. Coughlin's extremism became so intense as the years passed that he was eventually ordered to silence by his church authorities.[5]

Such demagogic attacks on Roosevelt took on a lunatic tinge with the passage of time, but one cannot ignore the large and impassioned following they won in appealing to widespread suffering and popular prejudice. Beyond easy solutions to desperate conditions, they tempted with the idea of revenge against the wealthy, who were responsible for the hard times. Had Roosevelt failed to alleviate the suffering and to inspire the hope that he did, how long the American democracy could resist the allure of promised panaceas is an unanswered question. The success of scapegoat ranting and promised prosperity had destroyed more fragile democracies in Europe. Americans took the wiser course.

The more long-established parties of the left, the Communists and Socialists, also drew some support in the United States, especially among the young, but they enjoyed no better fortune in trying to shake the country's confidence in Roosevelt. Despite all the plausible argument about the failure of capitalism, they fared even less well at the polls than the eccentrics. Socialist Norman Thomas, reasoned and moderate in his appeal for a new economic system, drew less than one-half of one percent of the vote for president in 1936. Communist candidate Earl Browder was even less attractive to American voters.

Demagogic figures like Long, Smith, and Coughlin represented one kind of danger; they were Jacobin types capable of the outrageous in the name of the people. Another kind of opposition, this from the right, was more enduring if less obviously threatening. The real counter-revolutionaries were those conservatives irreconcilable to progressive change, like a displaced aristocracy longing for the restoration of an ancien régime of laissez-faire capitalism. Theirs was the persistent hostility of a kind of American conservatism that wedded itself intimately to the interests of capital. From the Gilded Age through much of the 20th century, the defense of a libertarian laissez-faire economics submerged the more genuine and traditional ideals identified with conservative icons like Edmund Burke and John Adams.

Thus came the well-financed if electorally futile assaults on Roosevelt from the right. From the editorial boards to the corporate boards, the attacks were unrelenting. The working press was generally friendly and appreciative of the openness of Roosevelt, who held thousands of give-and-take press conferences. On the other hand, publishers like William Randolph Hearst with his multiple news outlets and Robert R. McCormick in the *Chicago Tribune* continually poured invective into their editorial forays against the un-American New Deal. The overwhelming majority of daily newspapers endorsed Alf Landon in 1936. In the case of the *Chicago Tribune*, the paper did not allow Roosevelt's name to appear on the front page for days at a time during the campaign.[6] Hostility from corporate interests, conservative Republicans, and their allies among the press moguls did not surprise. Roosevelt began his administration with a conscious effort at cooperation with business interests and was disappointed at the lack of cooperation and the depth of hostility from them. Once the lines were drawn, however, he was prepared for and even enjoyed doing battle. More difficult were the defections among some Democrats who rejected the New Deal as a dangerous turn in American politics. John W. Davis, Democratic candidate for president in 1924, when a desperate party tried to outdo the conservative appeal of Calvin Coolidge, described the New Deal as a form of despotism. John J. Raskob, former party chairman, official of DuPont and General Motors, and one of the builders of the Empire State Building, joined the chorus. These and others were quick to attack the New Deal as undermining the basic capitalist character of the United States with socialist ideas. Their language became as caustic as any Republican assault. The acknowledged leader of the renegade Democrats was Roosevelt's old ally, Alfred E. Smith.

Al Smith was never fully reconciled to being passed over for a second presidential run in 1932 and never quite forgave Roosevelt for displacing him. Although he did campaign for Roosevelt somewhat limply in 1932, he quickly developed a sharp antipathy to New Deal measures. By late 1933, he was describing the administration's actions as radical. In 1934, Smith took on the role of mouthpiece for the newly organized Liberty League. The League was formed in the summer of 1934 by Smith, Raskob, Davis, members of the Du Pont family, and other Democrats. Among these was Dean Acheson, perhaps in retaliation for his being fired as undersecretary of the Treasury in a dispute over administration economic policy. Beyond disaffected Democrats, the League drew much support from leaders of the nation's biggest corporations, including General Motors, U.S. Steel, Standard Oil, and Goodyear, and could eventually boast of over 200,000 members. The League orchestrated a drumbeat of criticism about the extreme character of Roosevelt's policies. The climax of the assault came at a dinner meeting at the Mayflower Hotel in Washington in January 1936, in anticipation of the fall presidential election. Al Smith was the featured speaker, and he abandoned all moderation.

The New Deal, he announced to a receptive audience, was promoting class warfare, a rant often repeated by the well-to-do against any administration bold enough to defend progressive taxation. Party loyalty was normally to be expected, but patriotism demanded that he attack the administration lodged in the White House, which he compared to the Kremlin. The government of the United States, which he likened to an octopus choking American business to death, was dominated by socialists. Ominously, he warned, "There can be only one atmosphere of government, the clear, pure fresh air of free America, or the foul breath of a communistic Russia." The sentiments were received with the most generous applause from this gathering of the nation's wealthiest. For his effort, Smith made a new admirer of an old enemy. The FDR-hating William Randolph Hearst offered editorial praise in his newspapers. Smith went on to support Landon in the election, adding to the political disappointments of his last years.[7]

Leaving the extreme quality of the charges against Roosevelt aside, the hostility of conservative elements in the United States took on a granite endurance fixed permanently in the political landscape. Roosevelt's coalition of support continued to produce Democratic victories in Congress and generally in the presidency for years, but conservative resistance to enlarging and completing New Deal designs never faltered. As noted, the cooperation of southern Democrats with Republicans made Democratic majorities less liberal than they appeared to be. That alliance hardened in the 1940s and made domestic politics difficult for Harry Truman. The success of the civil rights movement and federal guarantees of voting rights in the South eliminated the rationale for the politically solid South. As a result, droves of conservative Democrats in the South followed the lead of Strom Thurmond of South Carolina and found a more congenial political home in the Republican Party. These eventually contributed much to the cause of driving heretical moderates out of the party. Such conservatives continue to aim at repairing the damage done to the United States by Franklin Roosevelt.

8

The Legacy and the Challenge

Franklin Delano Roosevelt transformed the American democratic experiment with an economic and social revolution that added a new direction and purpose to government. From the start of the American experiment, government was assigned the role, not always successfully performed, of guaranteeing the freedom and essential equality of citizens. The Roosevelt revolution invested the government with the obligation and authority to promote the material well-being of citizens as a matter of human rights to which they were, at least implicitly, endowed by the Creator, as noted by the founders of the Republic. During the most active years of the New Deal, from 1933 to 1939, more work was devoted to improving the economic and social condition of the American people than in all the previous years of the nation's existence. Inevitably, the required tasks demanded an expanded federal government, even though much of the money spent and administration required moved through the states. The scale of programs and the sheer number of new federal agencies created a new kind of American government. It is truly remarkable, given the scope of activity and the enormous expenditures of money, how free of scandal the New Dealers remained. For many Americans this process generated a new attitude toward government as the solver of problems, an idea Ronald Reagan, once a strong supporter of the New Deal, later rejected by defining government as "the problem." Reagan's quip was a hard sell for folks whose monthly Social Security check was the difference between a dignified old age and penury.

William Leuchtenburg answers his own question, "What did the New Deal do?" with an impressive summary:

> It gave far greater amplitude to the national state, expanded the authority of the presidency, recruited university-trained administrators, won control of the money supply, established central banking, imposed regulation on Wall Street, monitored the air waves, rescued debt-ridden farmers and homeowners, built model communities, transformed homebuilding, made federal housing a permanent feature, fostered unionization of the factories, drastically reduced child labor, ended the tyranny of company towns, wiped out sweatshops, established minimal working standards, enabled thousands of tenants to buy their own farms, built camps for migrants, introduced the Welfare State with old-age pensions, unemployment insurance, and aid for dependent children and the handicapped, provided jobs for millions of unemployed, set up a special program for the jobless young and for students, covered the American landscape with new edifices, subsidized painters and novelists, composers and ballet dancers, introduced America's first state theater, created documentary films, gave birth to the impressive Tennessee Valley Authority, generated electric power, sent CCC boys into the forests, initiated the Soil Conservation Service, transformed the economy of agriculture, lighted up rural America, gave women greater recognition, made a start toward breaking the pattern of racial discrimination, put together a liberal party coalition, and changed the agenda of American politics.[1]

This Homeric recitation Leuchtenburg called an incomplete listing of New Deal contributions. Roosevelt's work became the model for successive progressive administrations to build on. Despite the waxing and waning of liberalism in American politics, the revolution was so firmly embraced as fundamentally American by so many people that, despite repeated conservative suggestions to the contrary, none have succeeded in its undoing.

As the role of government changed, there was a corresponding shift of emphasis from an intense individualism as a mythic source of national growth and greatness to the idea of communal action to establish a base for security and general well-being. Beyond recognizing the need for some elemental protection against the exigencies of age, infirmity, and economic hard times, Roosevelt also saw a role for government in protecting people from the more ravenous entrepreneurs who sought riches and power at the expense of the common interest, employing methods of dubious honesty and minimal equity.[2] He introduced a stronger measure of democracy to the economic system in rules to check capitalist abuses, in more equitable distributions of the fruits of national labor, and in giving ordinary people a greater sense of participation in the nation's destiny.

Communal action to solve community problems engenders an egalitarian spirit, and the New Deal was more egalitarian in spirit and action than any movement in American history, at least since the days of emancipation under Lincoln and of the expansion of popular suffrage during the age of Jackson. Mrs. Roosevelt often spoke and acted on behalf of African Americans and against ethnic as well as racial prejudice. She pointedly resigned her membership in the Daughters of the American Revolution when that organization denied the use of Constitution Hall for a concert by contralto Marian Anderson. Eleanor Roosevelt was often subjected to attacks because of her expressed sympathies for and friendship with African Americans. Elliot Roosevelt reports, "She took it as her moral duty to invite blacks into the White House, treat them as equals, have her picture taken with them, and argue their causes with father. He largely shared her concerns, but disagreed with her over the speed at which racial equality could be introduced."[3] In his New Deal struggle against the Depression and especially in getting long-term, permanent social reforms enacted, the president was confronted with the problem of winning the always tenuous support of southern senators and congressmen stuck firmly in the traditions of segregation and discrimination.

By 21st-century standards, race relations in the decade of the 1930s was still in the shadows of a dark age; but as uncompromising and dedicated an advocate of black rights as W. E. B. Du Bois conceded that blacks felt they had received more justice from Roosevelt than any president in recent memory, and he supported FDR in each of his elections. Black voters registered their approval and remained one of the most faithful elements in the Roosevelt electoral coalition. It has been argued that the improved economic condition of African Americans was an important element in the success of the civil rights movement in later years. The emphasis on civic and economic equality of opportunity added to the hatred of Roosevelt among the privileged and comfortable.[4]

What did the Roosevelt revolution do to capitalism? It saved it. Critics on the left, then and since, have wanted a more fundamental effort to change the system more dramatically than Roosevelt was willing to do. What a continuing failure to alleviate the suffering of a nation or to harness the unbridled power of the moneyed would have meant for the American economic and political system in the face of more radical impulses is speculative. But none of the best guesses appeal. The New Deal did not destroy the power of capital, nor did it stop the inexorable drift toward greater concentration among corporations, which remains a continuing concern. It did, however, subject the capitalist system to public regulation and forced capitalist enterprise to become more humane. In the process, it sustained a democratic society in an age when democracy was in retreat in many countries. By the end of the 1930s, most people in the industrialized world lived under authoritarian regimes. Roosevelt's work made both capitalism and democracy stronger and more secure in a world in which both were under assault.

In his message on the State of the Union[5] in January 1944, Roosevelt took some time away from war concerns to set the agenda for the future of his revolution. Here he tied together the three American revolutions by recognizing the connection between liberty and a minimal economic dignity. "We have come to the clear realization of the fact that true individual freedom cannot exist without economic security and independence." He spoke of

> a second Bill of Rights under which a new basis of security and prosperity can be established for all—regardless of station, race, or creed.
>
> Among these are:
>
> The right to a useful and remunerative job in industries or shops or farms or mines of the Nation;
>
> The right to earn enough to provide adequate food and clothing and recreation;
>
> The right of every farmer to raise and sell his products at a return which will give him and his family a decent living;
>
> The right of every businessman, large and small, to trade in an atmosphere of freedom from unfair competition and domination by monopolies at home or abroad;
>
> The right of every family to a decent home;
>
> The right to adequate medical care and the opportunity to achieve and enjoy good health;

The right to adequate protection from economic fears of old age, sickness, accident, and unemployment;
The right to a good education.

This, he said, was to be the work of the post-war United States. This went beyond assistance to those in desperate need to a promise of justice and dignity for every citizen. This was the unfinished business of the Roosevelt revolution. Like the work of Washington and Lincoln, realizing more fully the ideals established in each revolution required the work of future generations. The New Deal affirmed the ideals of economic equity and material security, and they remained indelible. After the war, Harry Truman fought for a "Fair Deal" and was frustrated by a powerful conservative alliance of southern Democrats and western Republicans. A surge of progressive legislation came with the Kennedy-Johnson Great Society years, and for a time measurable progress was made in reducing poverty and expanding health and other benefits for the elderly. But the American condition in the last decades of the 20th century was anticipated decades earlier by economist John Kenneth Galbraith, who lamented the combination of private affluence and public squalor that prevailed in the world's richest democracy.[6] The United States at the turn of the 21st century faced a deteriorating infrastructure, still awaited universal health care—advocated by Theodore Roosevelt as early as 1912—and still endured the embarrassment of entrenched poverty in a prosperous society.

A persistently conservative streak in American economic and political life was resurgent especially after 1970. As noted, that conservatism was far removed from traditional Burkean ideals of temperate change and stable institutions and was fully wedded to the acquisitive ideals of free-market capitalism. There developed a curious political mix of religion-driven social conservatism that also supported the deregulation of capitalist practices of a distinctly amoral acquisitive bent. If the social benefits of the New Deal could not be withdrawn, they certainly ought not to be extended. The conservative promise of uninterrupted prosperity for the diligent and a dogmatic identification of unfettered enterprise with "true Americanism" took hold with much of the electorate. The appeal was broad and the very word "liberal" became a pejorative label to be avoided by the ambitious politician. It was "morning in America." This was a seductive metaphor, but reality was more stark. Despite the righteous pronouncement that government was the problem and liberal spending was out of control, the growth of government in these years was unabated, and spending was profligate under the administrations of Ronald Reagan and the younger Bush, with little remedial effect on poverty or rotting infrastructure. There were, however, generous tax cuts for the highest incomes and sterling rewards for the speculating classes.

And so fulfilling the ideals of the Roosevelt revolution was set on hold, awaiting a new progressive mindset. The economic shocks of 2008 exposed the abysmal venality of the financial manipulators, now liberated by the repeal of key New Deal regulations and the negligent enforcement of those still in effect. With echoes of the debacle of 1929, collapsing financial institutions and tumbling stock values seemed eerily familiar. Perhaps those shocks, and a new generation of leadership, will renew the determination to resume the work of completing the Roosevelt revolution. The agenda is not mysterious. Equitable tax and distributive policy could end the entrenched poverty that shames this rich democracy. A society that can afford obscene levels of reward for the often mediocre performance of corporate executives [we often mistakenly associate the accumulation of wealth with the exercise of intelligence] should be able to support an effective system of universal health care. Those two objectives alone would do much to reflect and advance Roosevelt's design.

Roosevelt identified meaningful liberty in a democracy with a humane base of economic security. He sought that liberation from want and economic anxiety that would enable individuals, families, and communities to grow and flourish and to realize more fully their material and spiritual potential. Guided by the American example, 18th-century French revolutionaries coined "liberty, equality and fraternity" as the goals of their revolution. They failed, and quickly succumbed to the authoritarian temptation. The Americans did better in achieving the ideals imbedded in their original revolution. The revolutions of Washington and Lincoln proclaimed American liberty and equality, and succeeding generations helped to fulfill those objectives. Franklin Roosevelt showed the way to the third revolutionary goal— fraternity. His revolution awaits its full realization.

Franklin Delano Roosevelt. Courtesy of FDR Presidential Library.

FDR with his graduating class at Groton, 1900. Courtesy of FDR Presidential Library.

Assistant Secretary of the Navy Roosevelt with Woodrow Wilson, Flag Day, 1913. Courtesy of FDR Presidential Library.

Governor Roosevelt with Al Smith. Courtesy of FDR Presidential Library.

FDR and Herbert Hoover, Inauguration Day, March 4, 1933. Courtesy of FDR
Presidential Library.

FDR and son James greeting well-wishers, 1934. Courtesy of FDR Presidential Library.

CCC camp in California, 1933. Courtesy of FDR Presidential Library.

Signing the Social Security Act, 1935. Courtesy of Library of Congress.

Unemployed workers signing up for benefits, 1936. Courtesy of FDR Presidential Library.

9

Franklin D. Roosevelt— Philosophy of Government

The political and moral philosophy that impelled the Roosevelt revolution emerged quite clearly in the speeches and state papers delivered at key moments in FDR's presidential career. That philosophy reflected his fidelity to the ideals of the founding fathers, to the vision of Lincoln, and to his own lifelong political and religious commitments. From his days as governor and presidential candidate to his last State of the Union address in 1944, Roosevelt delivered a consistent vision of a humane democracy.

Roosevelt understood that the impact of the Industrial Revolution and the resulting transition from an overwhelmingly rural to a dominantly urban society required a recasting of the role of government, especially in matters economic. The explosion of industrial and finance capitalism in the 19th century forged new arrangements of power and influence and presented new problems of equity and justice in a democratic society. The freewheeling character of business enterprise designed by and for the engineers of capital was quickly defended as sacrosanct by the economic elites who profited hugely. Roosevelt did not share the conviction. He was repeatedly critical of business and political leaders who remained wedded to a Gilded Age economic and social vision now outworn and dangerous. He warned against such intense concentration of wealth that enabled the exercise of excessive private power by the owners of capital over the lives of others and over public affairs. Economic dynasties born of modern capitalism threatened a new despotism over working people. Such powerful interests created a class of privilege that Roosevelt thought antithetical to a democratic society.

Heir to the initiatives of Theodore Roosevelt and Woodrow Wilson in their early response to the realities of modern capitalist influence, FDR saw the necessity of countervailing government action to harness the power of capital while maintaining a respect for private initiative. He saw the responsibility of government to contribute to that economic security and justice essential to "the general welfare." There was no threat to individual liberty in this. On the contrary, he argued that real freedom and a secure democracy demanded a measure of broad economic well-being. He respected the dignity of honest labor and believed it was invested with spiritual value. For Roosevelt these political and economic imperatives were rooted in a progressive vision of democratic society and in his consistent religious commitment, especially to his traditional understanding of the virtue of charity. This vision served throughout his presidency as the template for the Roosevelt revolution.

The Social Age
Phi Beta Kappa Address
Harvard University—June 17, 1929

THE SOCIAL AGE—PHI BETA KAPPA ADDRESS

Harvard University, June 17, 1929

At the 25th reunion of his graduating class, Roosevelt delivered the prestigious Phi Beta Kappa Address. He offered a knowledgeable review of the progress of Western civilization from the ancient Greeks to the modern age. Searching for a key to the contemporary era, he labeled it the age of social consciousness. He applauded the progress and increasing egalitarianism of the times and a new sense of communal obligation more in tune with the teachings of religion. These obligations fell not only on churches and private individuals, but on the government as well. There are clues here to the sensibilities that would inform his political philosophy.

During the war, Mr. Lloyd-George said to me, "I will give a handsome prize to any imaginative American who will invent for me a new word to take the place of that overworked and unsatisfactory expression 'cooperation.' His search has borne no fruit and our language is still unable simply to express the thought of coordination of effort on the part of millions of human beings.

In like manner, it is impossible adequately in few words to give name to the age in which we live. Every era of human history is worthy of characterization, even though our historical terminology is based too largely on the names of men and of places, rather than on great trends of civilization.

To ask ourselves what is the trend of today may provoke disagreement and discussion, but it may serve to bring out new thoughts and perhaps enrich the English language. At least we may agree that the past 50 years have brought such unusual and far-reaching changes in the condition of life and the mental outlook of the world population that future generations will recognize this period as worthy at least of a name.

* * *

While I must use it as a temporary expedient, as the word "cooperation" was used during the World War, I incline to the phrase "The Age
of Social Consciousness" as most fitting the trend of our own day. It
best describes the change in the social relationships.

This broad current falls into two main channels. First, the very definite breaking down of the remnants of hereditary caste, and the plac-
ing of men and women on a closer comparable and competitive basis.
The Kansas farmer and the New York mechanic send their sons and
their daughters to college; there is a motor car for one out of every
four of the inhabitants of the United States; proper sanitation, excellent transportation, electric light, music, art, books by the million, the
news of the day, clothing, ready made food—all these are literally at
the command of the majority of our citizens. The luxuries of the past
generation are become the necessities of the present; in creature comforts, the making easy of daily household, we have gained more in 50
years than in the previous five centuries.

In the vocations of life, also the conditions surrounding work—
clerical and manual—are shown a steady rise to shorter hours and more
healthful surroundings; and in the field of avocations, the most note-
worthy change has been the discovery of recreational sports and out-
door play for the benefit of the city-dwelling men, women and children.
The point of emphasis is that in all of this what used to be the privileges
of the few has [sic] come to be the accepted heritage of the many.

A century and a half ago our forefathers spoke in theoretical terms
of equality, meaning thereby more particularly the equality of right.
Much later came the ideal of the equality of opportunity, and it has
been only in these latter years that we have seen, at least in part, its
realization.

In this aspect, the social consciousness of this age makes constant
strides. In all material particulars, the changes and importance are
weighed in their relationship to the good of the community; and even
though there be glaring instances of individual or group selfishness,
dishonesty in high places, and, of late, a tendency towards the concentration of material power into the hands of the few, yet, nevertheless,
the term "My Neighbor" is made to apply for more to fellow men and
women, rich and poor, Jew and Gentile, than it did in the days gone by
when "My Neighbor" meant one's personal friends and associates and
the members of one's own sect.

In the other stream, modern social consciousness has entered a wholly
new phase. We have evolved community obligations undreamed of

100 years ago. The State, the church and associations of private citizens have undertaken the definite care of the sick, the crippled and the mentally deficient. We are reaching far into more difficult problems. . . . We are investigating and stamping out the causes of disease and we are eliminating duplication and waste in production. More and more we are proving that modern conditions require the world instead of merely national point of view.

In this same catalogue fall the strides made in the past decade toward the ultimate avoidance of armed conflict. It is based just as much on the better understood economics of mankind as it is on the spiritual outlook.

The goal of the social consciousness of our today is a worthy goal. It conforms I think more truly to the teachings of religion than any objective of previous centuries. That it has its pitfalls and dangers is undeniable; that it may lead to a complexity of life which will drive mankind to a revolt in favor of a simpler existence is possible; that the same complexities may demand so much over-organization, enormously increased power over human beings will be narrowed into the hands of a new type of oligarchy is a danger of the future; that the strain of our daily doings may so weaken our material and physical fibre, that so-called less civilized races may replace the present dominant nations is also a potentiality for our grandchildren's day. Nevertheless, this age of social consciousness is with us now. We are married to it for better or worse; we are part of it and whatever may be our doubts or fears, we can do no good to our fellow men by sitting idly by or to seek to dam the current with a brick. Rather it is our privilege to help direct the ultimate course. In so doing we can be guided by two lessons of the past: first, the recorded history of the human race, showing the causes and effects of the influences behind that upward growth of civilization; secondly, simpler moralities which have been true of all the centuries.

THE COUNTRY NEEDS, THE COUNTRY DEMANDS BOLD, PERSISTENT EXPERIMENTATION

Oglethorpe University, May 22, 1932

This graduation address served the presidential campaign as Roosevelt forecast the spirit of what became the New Deal. He reflected on the collapse of optimistic hopes of the recent past and emphasized the need for national planning in that time of crisis. FDR here rejected the laissez-faire prescriptions of conservatives who suggested that the economic machine would right itself without needless tampering with traditional economic laws. After successive years of economic malaise, the call for action resonated with his audience.

For me as for you, this is a day of honorable attainment. For the honor conferred upon me I am deeply grateful, and I felicitate you upon yours, even though I cannot share with you that greater satisfaction which comes from a laurel worked for and won. For many of you, doubtless, this mark of distinction which you have received today has meant greater sacrifice by your parents or by yourselves, than you anticipated when you matriculated almost four years ago. The year 1928 does not seem far in the past, but since that time, as all of us are aware, the world about us has experienced significant changes. Four years ago, if you heard and believed the tidings of the time, you could expect to take your place in a society well supplied with material things and could look forward to the not-too-distant time when you would be living in your own homes, each (if you believed the politicians) with a two-car garage and, without great effort, would be providing yourselves and your families with all the necessities and amenities of life, and perhaps in addition, assure by your savings their security and your own in the future. Indeed, if you were observant, you would have seen that many of your elders had discovered a still easier road to material success. They had found that once they had accumulated a few dollars they needed only to put them in the proper place and then sit back and read in comfort the hieroglyphics called stock quotations which proclaimed that their wealth was mounting miraculously without any work or effort on their part. Many who were called and who are still pleased to call themselves the leaders of finance celebrated and assured us of an eternal future for this easy-chair mode of living. And to the stimulation of belief in this dazzling chimera were lent not only the voices of some of our public men in high office, but their influence and the material aid of the very instruments of Government which they controlled.

How sadly different is the picture which we see around us today! If only the mirage had vanished, we should not complain, for we should all be better off. But with it have vanished, not only the easy gains of speculation, but much of the savings of thrifty and prudent men and women, put by for their old age and for the education of their children. With these savings has gone, among millions of our fellow citizens, that sense of security to which they have rightly felt they are entitled in a land abundantly endowed with natural resources and with productive facilities to convert them into the necessities of life for all of our population. More calamitous still, there has vanished with the expectation of future security the certainty of today's bread and clothing and shelter.

* * *

You have been struck, I know, by the tragic irony of our economic situation today. We have not been brought to our present state by any natural calamity—by drought or floods or earthquakes, or by the destruction of our productive machine or our manpower. Indeed, we have a superabundance of raw materials, a more than ample supply of equipment for manufacturing these materials into the goods which we need, and transportation and commercial facilities for making them available to all who need them. But raw materials stand unused, factories stand idle, railroad traffic continues to dwindle, merchants sell less and less, while millions of able-bodied men and women, in dire need, are clamoring for the opportunity to work. This is the awful paradox with which we are confronted, a stinging rebuke that challenges our power to operate the economic machine which we have created.

We are presented with a multitude of views as to how we may again set into motion that economic machine. Some hold to the theory that the periodic slowing down of our economic machine is one of its inherent peculiarities—a peculiarity which we must grin, if we can, and bear because if we attempt to tamper with it we shall cause even worse ailments. According to this theory, as I see it, if we grin and bear long enough, the economic machine will eventually begin to pick up speed and in the course of an indefinite number of years will again attain that maximum number of revolutions which signifies what we have been wont to miscall prosperity, but which, alas, is but a last ostentatious twirl of the economic machine before it again succumbs to that mysterious impulse to slow down again. This attitude toward our economic machine requires not only greater stoicism, but greater faith in immutable economic law and less faith in the ability of man to control what he has created than I, for one, have. Whatever elements of truth lie in it, it is an invitation to sit back and do nothing; and all of us are suffering today, I believe, because this comfortable theory was too thoroughly implanted in the minds of some of our leaders, both in finance and in public affairs.

Other students of economics trace our present difficulties to the ravages of the World War and its bequest of unsolved political and economic and financial problems. Still others trace our difficulties to defects in the world's monetary systems. Whether it be an original cause, an accentuating cause, or an effect, the drastic change in the value of our monetary unit in terms of the commodities is a problem which we must meet straightforwardly. It is self-evident that we must either restore commodities to a level approximating their dollar value of several years ago or else that we must continue the destructive process of reducing, through defaults or through deliberate writing down, obligations assumed at a higher price level.

* * *

I believe that we are at the threshold of a fundamental change in our popular economic thought, that in the future we are going to think less about the producer and more about the consumer. Do what we may have to do to inject life into our ailing economic order, we cannot make it endure for long unless we can bring about a wiser, more equitable distribution of the national income.

It is well within the inventive capacity of man, who has built up this great social and economic machine capable of satisfying the wants of all, to insure that all who are willing and able to work receive from it at least the necessities of life. In such a system, the reward for a day's work will have to be greater, on the average, than it has been, and the reward to capital, especially capital which is speculative, will have to be less. But I believe that, after the experience of the last three years, the average citizen would rather receive a smaller return upon his savings in return for greater security for the principal, than experience for a moment the thrill or the prospect of being a millionaire only to find the next moment that his fortune, actual or expected, has withered in his hand because the economic machine has again broken down.

It is toward that objective that we must move if we are to profit by our recent experiences. Probably few will disagree that the goal is desirable. Yet many, of faint heart, fearful of change, sitting tightly on the rooftops in the flood, will sternly resist striking out for it, lest they fail to attain it. Even among those who are ready to attempt the journey there will be violent differences of opinion as to how it should be made. So complex, so widely distributed over our whole society are the problems which confront us that men and women of common aim do not agree upon the method of attacking them. Such disagreement leads to doing nothing, to drifting. Agreement may come too late.

Let us not confuse objectives with methods. Too many so-called leaders of the nation fail to see the forest because of the trees. Too many of them fail to recognize the vital necessity of planning for definite objectives. True leadership calls for the setting forth of the objectives and the rallying of public opinion in support of these objectives.

Do not confuse objectives with methods. When the nation becomes substantially united in favor of planning the broad objectives of civilization, then true leadership must unite thought behind definite methods.

The country needs and, unless I mistake its temper, the country demands bold, persistent experimentation. It is common sense to take a method and try it: If it fails, admit it frankly and try another. But above all, try something. The millions who are in want will not stand by silently forever while the things to satisfy their needs are within easy reach.

We need enthusiasm, imagination and the ability to face facts, even unpleasant ones, bravely. We need to correct, by drastic means if necessary, the faults in our economic system from which we now suffer. We need the courage of the young. Yours is not the task of making your way in the world, but the task of remaking the world which you will find before you. May every one of us be granted the courage, the faith, and the vision to give the best that is in us to that remaking!

NOMINATION ACCEPTANCE SPEECH

Chicago, July 2, 1932

Roosevelt flew to Chicago to accept his nomination—a dramatic, precedent-breaking gesture to display his aptitude for bold action and, not incidentally, his physical vigor despite infirmity. He told the delegates he rejected the idea that America's choice lay between radicalism and reaction and linked his politics to Wilsonian progressivism. He pledged to deliver a federal response to Depression relief, and almost casually uttered the words "new deal," which the press would soon apply as the indelible label of his administration.

I appreciate your willingness after these six arduous days to remain here, for I know well the sleepless hours which you and I have had. I regret that I am late, but I have no control over the winds of heaven and could only be thankful for my Navy training.

The appearance before a National Convention of its nominee for President, to be formally notified of his selection, is unprecedented and unusual, but these are unprecedented and unusual times. I have started out on the tasks that lie ahead by breaking the absurd traditions that the candidate should remain in professed ignorance of what has happened for weeks until he is formally notified of that event many weeks later.

My friends, may this be the symbol of my intention to be honest and to avoid all hypocrisy or sham, to avoid all silly shutting of the eyes to the truth in this campaign. You have nominated me and I know it, and I am here to thank you for the honor.

Let it also be symbolic that in so doing I broke traditions. Let it be from now on the task of our Party to break foolish traditions. We will break foolish traditions and leave it to the Republican leadership, far more skilled in that art, to break promises.

Let us now and here highly resolve to resume the country's interrupted march along the path of real progress, of real justice, of real equality for all of our citizens, great and small. Our indomitable leader in that interrupted march is no longer with us, but there still survives today his spirit. Many of his captains, thank God, are still with us, to give us wise counsel. Let us feel that in everything we do there still lives with us, if not the body, the great indomitable, unquenchable, progressive soul of our Commander-in-Chief, Woodrow Wilson. . . .

As we enter this new battle, let us keep always present with us some of the ideals of the Party: The fact that the Democratic Party by tradition and by the continuing logic of history, past and present, is the bearer of liberalism and of progress and at the same time of safety to our institutions. And if this appeal fails, remember well, my friends, that a resentment against the failure of Republican leadership—and note well that in this campaign I shall not use the word "Republican Party," but I shall use, day in and day out, the words, "Republican leadership"—the failure of Republican leaders to solve our troubles may degenerate into unreasoning radicalism.

The great social phenomenon of this depression, unlike others before it, is that it has produced but a few of the disorderly manifestations that too often attend upon such times.

Wild radicalism has made few converts, and the greatest tribute that I can pay to my countrymen is that in these days of crushing want there persists an orderly and hopeful spirit on the part of the millions of our people who have suffered so much. To fail to offer them a new chance is not only to betray their hopes but to misunderstand their patience.

To meet by reaction that danger of radicalism is to invite disaster. Reaction is no barrier to the radical. It is a challenge, a provocation. The way to meet that danger is to offer a workable program of reconstruction, and the party to offer it is the party with clean hands.

This, and this only, is a proper protection against blind reaction on the one hand and an improvised, hit-or-miss, irresponsible opportunism on the other.

There are two ways of viewing the government's duty in matters affecting economic and social life. The first sees to it that a favored few are helped and hopes that some of their prosperity will leak through, sift through, to labor, to the farmer, to the small business man. That theory belongs to the party of Toryism, and I had hoped that most of the Tories left this country in 1776.

But it is not and never will be the theory of the Democratic Party. This is no time for fear, for reaction or for timidity. Here and now, I invite those nominal Republicans who find that their conscience cannot be squared with the groping and the failure of their party leaders to join hands with us; here and now, in equal measure, I warn those nominal Democrats who squint at the future with their faces turned toward the past, and who feel no responsibility to the demands of the new time, that they are out of step with their Party.

Yes, the people of this country want a genuine choice this year, not a choice between two names for the same reactionary doctrine. Ours must be a party of liberal thought, of planned action, of enlightened international outlook, and of the greatest good to the greatest number of our citizens.

Now it is inevitable—and the choice is that of the times—it is inevitable that the main issue of this campaign should revolve about the clear fact of our economic condition, a depression so deep that it is without precedent in modern history. It will not do merely to state, as do Republican leaders to explain their broken promises of continued inaction, that the depression is worldwide. That was not their explanation of the apparent prosperity of 1928. The people will not forget the claim made by them then that prosperity was only a domestic product manufactured by a Republican President and a Republican Congress. If they claim paternity for the one they cannot deny paternity for the other.

* * *

Out of all the tons of printed paper, out of all the hours of oratory, the recriminations, the defenses, the happy-thought plans in Washington and in every state, there emerges one great, simple, crystal-pure fact that, during the past ten years, a nation of 120 million people has been led by the Republican leaders to erect an impregnable barbed wire entanglement around its borders through the instrumentality of tariffs which have isolated us from all the other human beings in all the rest of the round world. I accept that admirable tariff statement in the platform of this convention. It would protect American business and American labor. By our acts of the past, we have invited and received the retaliation of other Nations. I propose an invitation to them to forget the past, to sit at the table with us, as friends, and to plan with us for the restoration of the trade of the world.

Go into the home of the business man. He knows what the tariff has done for him. Go into the home of the factory worker. He knows why goods do not move. Go into the home of the farmer. He knows how the tariff has helped to ruin him.

At last, our eyes are open. At last, the American people are ready to acknowledge that Republican leadership was wrong and that the Democracy is right.

My program, of which I can only touch on these points, is based upon this simple moral principle: the welfare and the soundness of a nation depend first upon what the great mass of the people wish and need; and second, whether or not they are getting it.

What do the people of America want more than anything else? To my mind, they want two things: work, with all the moral and spiritual values that go with it; and with work, a reasonable measure of security—security for themselves and for their wives and children. Work and security—these are more than words. They are more than facts. They are the spiritual values, the true goal toward which our efforts of reconstruction should lead. These are the values that this program is intended to gain; these are the values we have failed to achieve by the leadership we now have.

Our Republican leaders tell us economic laws—sacred, inviolable, unchangeable—cause panics which no one could prevent. But while they prate of economic laws, men and women are starving. We must lay hold of the fact that economic laws are not made by nature. They are made by human beings.

Yes, when—not if—when we get the chance, the federal government will assume bold leadership in distress relief. For years, Washington has alternated between putting its head in the sand and saying there is no large number of destitute people in our midst who need food and clothing, and then saying the states should take care of them, if there are. Instead of planning two and a half years ago to do what they are now trying to do, they kept putting it off from day to day, week to week, and month to month, until the conscience of America demanded action.

I say that while primary responsibility for relief rests with localities now, as ever, yet the federal government has always had and still has a continuing responsibility for the broader public welfare. It will soon fulfill that responsibility. . . .

One word more: Out of every crisis, every tribulation, every disaster, mankind rises with some share of greater knowledge, of higher decency, of purer purpose. Today we shall have come through a period of loose thinking, descending morals, an era of selfishness, among individual men and women and among nations. Blame not governments alone for this. Blame ourselves in equal share. Let us be frank in acknowledgment of the truth that many amongst us have made obeisance to Mammon, that the profits of speculation, the easy road without toil, have lured us from the old barricades. To return to higher standards we must abandon the false prophets and seek new leaders of our own choosing.

Never before in modern history have the essential differences between the two major American parties stood out in such striking contrast as they do today. Republican leaders not only have failed in material things, they have failed in national vision, because in disaster they have held out no hope, they have pointed out no path for the people below to climb back to places of security and of safety in our American life.

Throughout the nation, men and women, forgotten in the political philosophy of the government of the last years, look to us here for guidance and for more equitable opportunity to share in the distribution of national wealth.

On the farms, in the large metropolitan areas, in the smaller cities and in the villages, millions of our citizens cherish the hope that their old standards of living and of thought have not gone forever. Those millions cannot and shall not hope in vain.

I pledge you, I pledge myself, to a new deal for the American people. Let us all here assembled constitute ourselves prophets of a new order of competence and of courage. This is more than a political campaign; it is a call to arms. Give me your help, not to win votes alone, but to win in this crusade to restore America to its own people.

COMMONWEALTH CLUB ADDRESS

San Francisco, September 23, 1932

This important campaign address enunciated Roosevelt's philosophy of government. Roosevelt paid tribute to the founding fathers and identified himself as a Jeffersonian without Jefferson's small-government prejudice. It was the Industrial Revolution that required a new assessment of the role of government. His reading of American history contrasted business resistance to government regulation with its willingness to accept and encourage government protection and subsidy. He emphasized the dangers of concentrated economic power and called for a "reappraisal of values" and a balanced role for government in providing both necessary regulation and protecting liberty.

I count it a privilege to be invited to address the Commonwealth Club. It has stood in the life of this city and state, and it is perhaps accurate to add, the nation, as a group of citizen leaders interested in fundamental problems of government, and chiefly concerned with achievement of progress in government through non-partisan means. The privilege of addressing you, therefore, in the heat of a political campaign, is great. I want to respond to your courtesy in terms consistent with your policy.

* * *

The issue of government has always been whether individual men and women will have to serve some system of government of economics, or whether a system of government and economics exists to serve individual men and women. This question has persistently dominated the discussion of government for many generations. On questions relating to these things, men have differed, and for time immemorial it is probable that honest men will continue to differ. . . .

When we look about us, we are likely to forget how hard people have worked to win the privilege of government. The growth of the national governments of Europe was a struggle for the development of a centralized force in the nation, strong enough to impose peace upon ruling barons. In many instances, the victory of the central government, the creation of a strong central government, was a haven of refuge to the individual. The people preferred the master far away to the exploitation and cruelty of the smaller master near at hand.

But the creators of national government were perforce ruthless men. They were often cruel in their methods, but they did strive steadily toward something that society needed and very much wanted, a strong central state, able to keep the peace, to stamp out civil war, to put the unruly nobleman in his place, and to permit the bulk of individuals to live safely. The man of ruthless force had his place in developing a pioneer country, just as he did in fixing the power of the central government in the development of nations. Society paid him well for his services and its development. When the development among the nations of Europe, however, has been completed, ambition, and ruthlessness, having served its term tended to overstep its mark.

There came a growing feeling that government was conducted for the benefit of a few who thrived unduly at the expense of all. The people sought a balancing—a limiting force. There came gradually, through town councils, trade guilds, national parliaments, by constitution and by popular participation and control, limitations on arbitrary power.

Another factor that tended to limit the power of those who ruled was the rise of the ethical conception that a ruler bore a responsibility for the welfare of his subjects.

The American colonies were born in this struggle. The American Revolution was a turning point in it. After the revolution, the struggle continued and shaped itself in the public life of the country. There were those who because they had seen the confusion which attended the years of war for American independence surrendered to the belief that popular government was essentially dangerous and essentially unworkable. They were honest people, my friends, and we cannot deny that their experience had warranted some measure of fear. The most brilliant, honest and able exponent of this point of view was Hamilton. He was too impatient of slow-moving methods. Fundamentally, he believed that the safety of the republic lay in the autocratic strength of its government, that the destiny of individuals was to serve that government, and that fundamentally a great and strong group of central institutions, guided by a small group of able and public-spirited citizens, could best direct all government.

But Mr. Jefferson, in the summer of 1776, after drafting the Declaration of Independence, turned his mind to the same problem and took a different view. He did not deceive himself with outward forms. Government to him was a means to an end, not an end in itself; it might be either a refuge and a help or a threat and a danger, depending on the circumstances. We find him carefully analyzing the society for which he was to organize a government. "We have no paupers. The great mass of our population is of laborers, our rich who cannot live without labor, either manual or professional, being few and of moderate wealth. Most of the laboring class possess property, cultivate their own lands, have families and from the demand for their labor, are enabled to exact from the rich and the competent such prices as enable them to feed abundantly, clothe above mere decency, to labor moderately and raise their families."

These people, he considered, had two sets of rights, those of "personal competency" and those involved in acquiring and possessing property. By "personal competency," he meant the right of free thinking, freedom of forming and expressing opinions, and freedom of personal living each man according to his own lights. To insure the first set of rights, a government must so order its functions as not to interfere with the individual. But even Jefferson realized that the exercise of the property rights might so interfere with the rights of the individual that the government, without whose assistance the property rights could not exist, must intervene, not to destroy individualism but to protect it.

You are familiar with the great political duel which followed, and how Hamilton, and his friends, building towards a dominant centralized power, were at length defeated in the great election of 1800, by Mr. Jefferson's party. Out of that duel came the two parties, Republican and Democratic, as we know them today.

So began, in American political life, the new day, the day of the individual against the system, the day in which individualism was made the great watchword of American life. The happiest of economic conditions made that day long and splendid. On the western frontier, land was substantially free. No one, who did not shirk the task of earning a living, was entirely without opportunity to do so. Depressions could, and did, come and go; but they could not alter the fundamental fact that most of the people lived partly by selling their labor and partly by extracting their livelihood from the soil, so that starvation and dislocation were practically impossible. At the very worst there was always the possibility of climbing into a covered wagon and moving west where the untilled prairies afforded a haven for men to whom the East did not provide a place. So great were our natural resources that we could offer this relief not only to our own people, but to the distressed of all the world; we could invite immigration from Europe, and welcome it with open arms. Traditionally, when a depression came, a new section of land was opened in the West; and even our temporary misfortune served our manifest destiny.

It was the middle of the 19th century that a new force was released and a new dream created. The force was what is called the Industrial Revolution, the advance of steam and machinery and the rise of the forerunners of the modern industrial plant. The dream was the dream of an economic machine, able to raise the standard of living for everyone; to bring luxury within the reach of the humblest; to annihilate distance by steam power and later by electricity; and to release everyone from the drudgery of the heaviest manual toil. It was to be expected that this would necessarily affect government. Heretofore, government had merely been called upon to produce conditions within which people could live happily, labor peacefully, and rest secure. Now it was called upon to aid in the consummation of this new dream. There was, however, a shadow over the dream. To be made real, it required use of the talents of men of tremendous will, and tremendous ambition, since by no other force could the problems of financing and engineering and new developments be brought to a consummation.

So manifest were the advantages of the machine age, however, that the United States fearlessly, cheerfully, and, I think, rightly, accepted the bitter with the sweet. It was thought that no price was too high to pay for the advantages which we could draw from a finished industrial system. The history of the last half century is accordingly in large measure a history of a group of financial titans, whose methods were not scrutinized with too much care, and who were honored in proportion as they produced the results, irrespective of the means they used. The financiers who pushed the railroads to the Pacific were always ruthless, we have them today. It has been estimated that the American investor paid for the American railway system more than three times over in the process; but despite that fact the net advantage was to the United States. As long as we had free land; as long as population was growing by leaps and bounds; as long as our industrial plants were insufficient to supply our needs, society chose to give the ambitious man free play and unlimited reward provided only that he produced the economic plant so much desired.

During this period of expansion, there was equal opportunity for all and the business of government was not to interfere but to assist in the development of industry. This was done at the request of businessmen themselves. The tariff was originally imposed for the purpose of "fostering our infant industry," a phrase I think the older among you will remember as a political issue not so long ago. The railroads were subsidized, sometimes by grants of money, oftener by grants of land; some of the most valuable oil lands in the United States were granted to assist the financing of the railroad which pushed through the Southwest. A nascent merchant marine was assisted by grants of money, or by mail subsidies, so that our steam shipping might ply the seven seas. Some of my friends tell me that they do not want the government in business. With this I agree; but I wonder whether they realize the implications of the past. For while it has been American doctrine that the government must not go into business in competition with private enterprises, still it has been traditional particularly in Republican administrations for business urgently to ask the government to put at private disposal all kinds of government assistance.

The same man who tells you that he does not want to see the government interfere in business—and he means it, and has plenty of good reasons for saying so—is the first to go to Washington and ask the government for a prohibitory tariff on his product. When things get just bad enough—as they did two years ago—he will go with equal speed to the United States government and ask for a loan; and the Reconstruction Finance Corporation is the outcome of it. Each group has sought protection from the government for its own special interest, without realizing that the function of government must be to favor no small group at the expense of its duty to protect the rights of personal freedom and of private property of all its citizens.

In retrospect, we can now see that the turn of the tide came with the turn of the century. We were reaching our last frontier; there was no more free land and our industrial combinations had become great uncontrolled and irresponsible units of power within the state. Clear-sighted men saw with fear the danger that opportunity would no longer be equal; that the growing corporation, like the feudal baron of old, might threaten the economic freedom of individuals to earn a living. In that hour, our antitrust laws were born. The cry was raised against the great corporations. Theodore Roosevelt, the first great Republican progressive, fought a presidential campaign on the issue of "trust busting" and talked freely about malefactors of great wealth. If the government had a policy it was rather to turn the clock back, to destroy the large combinations and to return to the time when every man owned his individual small business.

This was impossible; Theodore Roosevelt, abandoning the idea of "trust busting," was forced to work out a difference between "good" trusts and "bad" trusts. The Supreme Court set forth the famous "rule of reason" by which it seems to have meant that a concentration of industrial power was permissible if the method by which it got its power, and the use it made of that power, was reasonable.

Woodrow Wilson, elected in 1912, saw the situation more clearly. Where Jefferson had feared the encroachment of political power on the lives of individuals, Wilson knew that the new power was financial. He saw, in the highly centralized economic system, the despot of the 20th century, on whom great masses of individuals relied for their safety and their livelihood, and whose irresponsibility and greed (if it were not controlled) would reduce them to starvation and penury. The concentration of financial power had not proceeded so far in 1912 as it has today; but it had grown far enough for Mr. Wilson to realize fully its implications. It is interesting, now, to read his speeches.

What is called "radical" today (and I have reason to know whereof I speak) is mild compared to the campaign of Mr. Wilson. "No man can deny," he said, "that the lines of endeavor have more and more narrowed and stiffened; no man who knows anything about the development of industry in this country can have failed to observe that the larger kinds of credit are more and more difficult to obtain unless you obtain them upon terms of uniting your efforts with those who already control the industry of the country, and nobody can fail to observe that every man who tries to set himself up in competition with any process of manufacture which has taken place under the control of large combinations of capital will presently find himself either squeezed out or obliged to sell and allow himself to be absorbed."

Had there been no World War—had Mr. Wilson been able to devote eight years to domestic instead of to international affairs—we might have had a wholly different situation at the present time. However, the then distant roar of European cannon, growing ever louder, forced him to abandon the study of this issue. The problem he saw so clearly is left with us as a legacy; and no one of us on either side of the political controversy can deny that it is a matter of grave concern to the government.

A glance at the situation today only too clearly indicates that equality of opportunity as we have known it no longer exists. Our industrial plant is built; the problem just now is whether under existing conditions it is not overbuilt. Our last frontier has long since been reached, and there is practically no more free land. More than half of our people do not live on the farms or on lands and cannot derive a living by cultivating their own property. There is no safety valve in the form of a western prairie to which those thrown out of work by the eastern economic machines can go for a new start. We are not able to invite the immigration from Europe to share our endless plenty. We are now providing a drab living for our own people.

* * *

Recently a careful study was made of the concentration of business in the United States. It showed that our economic life was dominated by some 600 odd corporations who controlled two-thirds of American industry. Ten million small business men divided the other third. More striking still, it appeared that if the process of concentration goes on at the same rate, at the end of another century we shall have all American industry controlled by a dozen corporations, and run by perhaps a hundred men. Put plainly, we are steering a steady course toward economic oligarchy, if we are not there already.

Clearly, all this calls for a re-appraisal of values. A mere builder of more industrial plants, a creator of more railroad systems, and organizer of more corporations, is as likely to be a danger as a help. The day of the great promoter or the financial Titan, to whom we granted anything if only he would build, or develop, is over. Our task now is not discovery or exploitation of natural resources, or necessarily producing more goods. It is the soberer, less dramatic business of administering resources and plants already in hand, of seeking to reestablish foreign markets for our surplus production, of meeting the problem of underconsumption, of adjusting production to consumption, of distributing wealth and products more equitably, of adapting existing economic organizations to the service of the people. The day of enlightened administration has come.

Just as in older times the central government was first a haven of refuge, and then a threat, so now in a closer economic system the central and ambitious financial unit is no longer a servant of national desire, but a danger. I would draw the parallel one step farther. We did not think because national government had become a threat in the 18th century that therefore we should abandon the principle of national government. Nor today should we abandon the principle of strong economic units called corporations, merely because their power is susceptible of easy abuse. In other times we dealt with the problem of an unduly ambitious central government by modifying it gradually into a constitutional democratic government. So today, we are modifying and controlling our economic units.

As I see it, the task of government in its relation to business is to assist the development of an economic declaration of rights, an economic constitutional order. This is the common task of statesman and business man. It is the minimum requirement of a more permanently safe order of things.

Every man has a right to life; and this means that he has also a right to make a comfortable living. He may by sloth or crime decline to exercise that right; but it may not be denied him. We have no actual famine or death; our industrial and agricultural mechanism can produce enough and to spare. Our government formal and informal, political and economic, owes to every one an avenue to possess himself of a portion of that plenty sufficient for his needs, through his own work.

Every man has a right to his own property; which means a right to be assured, to the fullest extent attainable, in the safety of his savings. By no other means can men carry the burdens of those parts of life which, in the nature of things, afford no chance of labor: childhood, sickness, old age. In all thought of property, this right is paramount; all other property rights must yield to it. If, in accord with this principle, we must restrict the operations of the speculator, the manipulator, even the financier, I believe we must accept the restriction as needful, not to hamper individualism but to protect it.

* * *

Faith in America, faith in our tradition of personal responsibility, faith in our institutions, faith in ourselves demands that we recognize the new terms of the old social contract. We shall fulfill them, as we fulfilled the obligation of the apparent Utopia which Jefferson imagined for us in 1776, and which Jefferson, Roosevelt and Wilson sought to bring to realization. We must do so, lest a rising tide of misery engendered by our common failure, engulf us all. But failure is not an American habit; and in the strength of great hope we must all shoulder our common load.

SOCIAL JUSTICE THROUGH SOCIAL ACTION

Campaign Address, Detroit, October 2, 1932

Harking back to action in the New York Assembly 20 years earlier, Roosevelt identified himself with the Progressive movement and with Woodrow Wilson. He contrasted a laissez-faire political philosophy with one committed to government-led social action. Emphasizing the moral imperative of social reform, he enlisted support from the words of leaders of the three principal religious groups in the United States.

You know today is Sunday, and I am afraid that some of you people today in Detroit have been talking politics. Well, I am not going to. I want to talk to you about government. That is a very different thing. And I am not going to refer to parties at all.

I am going to refer to some of the fundamentals that antedate parties, and antedate republics and empires, fundamentals that are as old as mankind itself. They are fundamentals that have been expressed in philosophies, for I don't know how many thousands of years, in every part of the world. Today, in our boasted modern civilization, we are facing just exactly the same problem, just exactly the same conflict between two schools of philosophy that they faced in the earliest days of America, and indeed of the world. One of them—one of these old philosophies—is the philosophy of those who would "let things alone." The other is the philosophy that strives for something new— something that the human race has never attained yet, but something which I believe the human race can and will attain—social justice, through social action.

From the days of the caveman to the days of the automobile, the philosophy of "letting things alone" has resulted in the jungle law of the survival of the so-called fittest. The philosophy of social action results in the protection of humanity and the fitting of as many human beings as possible into the scheme of surviving. I am sorry to say that among the followers of that first philosophy of "letting things alone" are a lot of people in my community back home, which is a little village, and in the farming districts of the nation and in the great cities, such as yours. We can place in that philosophy a great many splendid people who keep saying, not only to themselves and to their friends, but to the community as a whole, "Why shouldn't we 'let things alone?' In the first place they are not as bad as they are painted, and in the second place they will cure themselves. Time is a great healer." An easy philosophy! The kind of philosophy, my friends, that was expressed the other day by a Cabinet officer of the United States of America, when he is reported to have said, "Our children are apt to profit rather than suffer from what is going on."

While he was saying that, another branch of our government, the United States Public Health Service, which believes in my kind of philosophy, I think, said this: "Over six millions of our public school children do not have enough to eat. Many of them are fainting at their desks. They are a prey to disease. Their future health is menaced."

In which school do you believe?

* * *

I go back 22 years to a time when, in my State of New York, we tried to pass in the legislature what we called a Workmen's Compensation Act, knowing, as we did, that there were thousands of men and women who every year were seriously injured in industrial accidents of one kind or another, who became a burden on their community, who were unable to work, unable to get adequate medical care. A lot of us youngsters in the legislature in those days were called radicals. We were called Socialists. They did not know the word Bolshevik in those days, but if they had known that, we would have been called that, too. We put through a Workmen's Compensation Act. The courts, thinking in terms of the 17th century, as some courts do, declared it to be unconstitutional. So we had to go about amending the constitution, and the following year we got a Workmen's Compensation Act.

What has it done? We were not the first state to have it. One of the earliest states, by the way, was New Jersey, which, the year before the action in the State of New York, passed a Workmen's Compensation Act at the bidding of that great humanitarian Governor, Woodrow Wilson. The result has been that almost every state of the Union has eliminated that cause of poverty among the masses of the people.

* * *

Yes, the followers of the philosophy of "let alone" have been decrying all of these measures of social welfare. What do they call them? They call them "paternalistic." All right, if they are paternalistic, I am a father.

They maintain that these laws interfere with individualism, forgetful of the fact that the causes of poverty in the main are beyond the control of any one individual or any czar, either a czar of politics or a czar of industry. The followers of the philosophy of "social action for the prevention of poverty" maintain that if we set up a system of justice we shall have small need for the exercise of mere philanthropy. Justice, after all, is the first goal we seek. We believe that when justice has been done individualism will have a greater security to devote the best that individualism itself can give. In other words, my friends, our long-range objective is not a dole, but a job.

* * *

My friends, the ideal of social justice of which I have spoken—an ideal that years ago might have been thought over-advanced—is now accepted by the moral leadership of all of the great religious groups of the country. Radical? Yes, and I shall show you how radical it is. I am going to cite three examples of what the churches say, the radical churches of America—Protestant, Catholic and Jewish.

And first I will read to you from the Sunday Sermon, the Labor Sermon sent out this year by the Federal Council of Churches of Christ in America, representing a very large proportion of the Protestants in our country.

Hear how radical they are: They say: "The thing that matters in any industrial system is what it does actually to human beings. . . .

"It is not denied that many persons of wealth are rendering great service to society. It is only suggested that the wealthy are overpaid in sharp contrast with the underpaid masses of the people. The concentration of wealth carries with it a dangerous concentration of power. It leads to conflict and violence. To suppress the symptoms of this inherent conflict while leaving the fundamental causes of it untouched is neither sound statesmanship nor Christian good-will.

"It is becoming more and more clear that the principles of our religion and the findings of social sciences point in the same direction. Economists now call attention to the fact that the present distribution of wealth and income, which is so unbrotherly in the light of Christian ethics, is also unscientific in that it does not furnish purchasing power to the masses to balance consumption and production in our machine age."

And now I am going to read you another great declaration and I wonder how many people will call it radical. It is just as radical as I am. It is a declaration from one of the greatest forces of conservatism in the world, the Catholic Church. I quote, my friends, from the scholarly encyclical issued last year by the Pope, one of the greatest documents of modern times:

"It is patent in our days that not alone is wealth accumulated, but immense power and despotic economic domination are concentrated in the hands of a few, and that those few are frequently not the owners but only the trustees and directors of invested funds which they administer at their good pleasure. . . .

"This accumulation of power, the characteristic note of the modern economic order, is a natural result of limitless free competition, which permits the survival of those only who are the strongest, which often means those who fight most relentlessly, who pay least heed to the dictates of conscience.

"This concentration of power has led to a three-fold struggle for domination: First, there is the struggle for dictatorship in the economic sphere itself; then the fierce battle to acquire control of the Government, so that its resources and authority may be abused in the economic struggle, and, finally, the clash between the Governments themselves."

And finally, I would read to you from another great statement, a statement from Rabbi Edward L. Israel, Chairman of the Social Justice Commission of the Central Conference of American Rabbis. Here is what he says:

"We talk of the stabilization of business. What we need is the stabilization of human justice and happiness and the permanent employment of economic policies which will enable us to preserve the essential human values of life amid all the changing aspects of the economic order. We must have a revamping of the entire method of approach to these problems of the economic order. We need a new type of social conscience that will give us courage to act. . . .

"We so easily forget. Once the cry of so-called prosperity is heard in the land, we all become so stampeded by the spirit of the god Mammon, that we cannot serve the dictates of social conscience. . . . We are here to serve notice that the economic order is the invention of man; and that it cannot dominate certain eternal principles of justice and of God."

And so, my friends, I feel a little as if I had been preaching a sermon. I feel a little as if I had been talking too much of some of the fundamentals, and yet those fundamentals enter into your life and my life every day. More, perhaps, than we can realize. . . .

We need leadership, of course. We need leadership of people who are honest in their thinking and honest in their doing. We need leadership if it is straight thinking and unselfish; but in the last analysis we must have the help of the men and women all the way from the top to the bottom, especially of the men and women who believe in the school of philosophy which is not content to leave things as they are.

And so, in these days of difficulty, we Americans everywhere must and shall choose the path of social justice—the only path that will lead us to a permanent bettering of our civilization, the path that our children must tread and their children must tread, the path of faith, the path of hope and the path of love toward our fellow man.

FIRST INAUGURAL ADDRESS

March 4, 1933

The new president began his address with his often-quoted reassurance against crippling fear. He placed the blame for the nation's crisis squarely on the shoulders of the "money changers," and called for a revision of the ethical disposition of the country. Sustaining traditional moral values was more important than profit, and he invoked a rule of the social gospel that in time of need we should "minister to our fellow men." He accompanied that exhortation to ethical rededication with a call for prompt and decisive action, while also suggesting that effective action might require extraordinary executive power.

I am certain my fellow Americans expect that on my induction into the presidency I will address them with a candor and a decision which the present situation of our nation impels. This is preeminently the time to speak the truth, the whole truth, frankly and boldly. Nor need we shrink from honestly facing conditions in our country today. This great nation will endure as it has endured, will revive and will prosper. So, first of all, let me assert my firm belief that the only thing we have to fear is fear itself—nameless, unreasoning, unjustified terror which paralyzes needed efforts to convert retreat into advance. In every dark hour of our national life a leadership of frankness and vigor has met with that understanding and support of the people themselves which is essential to victory. I am convinced that you will again give that support to leadership in these critical days.

In such a spirit on my part and on yours, we face our common difficulties. They concern, thank God, only material things. Values have shrunken to fantastic levels; taxes have risen; our ability to pay has fallen; government of all kinds is faced by serious curtailment of income; the means of exchange are frozen in the currents of trade; the withered leaves of industrial enterprise lie on every side; farmers find no markets for their produce; the savings of many years in thousands of families are gone. More important, a host of unemployed citizens face the grim problem of existence, and an equally great number toil with little return. Only a foolish optimist can deny the dark realities of the moment.

Yet our distress comes from no failure of substance. We are stricken by no plague of locusts. Compared with the perils which our forefathers conquered because they believed and were not afraid, we have still much to be thankful for. Nature still offers her bounty and human efforts have multiplied it. Plenty is at our doorstep, but a generous use of it languishes in the very sight of the supply. Primarily this is because rulers of the exchange of mankind's goods have failed through their own stubbornness and their own incompetence, have admitted their failure, and have abdicated. Practices of the unscrupulous money-changers stand indicted in the court of public opinion, rejected by the hearts and minds of men.

True they have tried, but their efforts have been cast in the pattern of an outworn tradition. Faced by failure of credit they have proposed only the lending of more money. Stripped of the lure of profit by which to induce our people to follow their false leadership, they have resorted to exhortations, pleading tearfully for restored confidence. They know only the rules of a generation of self-seekers. They have no vision, and when there is no vision the people perish.

The moneychangers have fled from their high seats in the temple of our civilization. We may now restore that temple to the ancient truths. The measure of the restoration lies in the extent to which we apply social values more noble than mere monetary profit.

Happiness lies not in the mere possession of money; it lies in the joy of achievement, in the thrill of creative effort. The joy and moral stimulation of work no longer must be forgotten in the mad chase of evanescent profits. These dark days will be worth all they cost us if they teach us that our true destiny is not to be ministered unto but to minister to ourselves and to our fellow men.

Recognition of the falsity of material wealth as the standard of success goes hand in hand with the abandonment of the false belief that public office and high political position are to be valued only by the standards of pride of place and personal profit; and there must be an end to a conduct in banking and in business which too often has given to a sacred trust the likeness of callous and selfish wrongdoing. Small wonder that confidence languishes, for it thrives only on honesty, on honor, on the sacredness of obligations, on faithful protection, on unselfish performance; without them it cannot live.

Restoration calls, however, not for changes in ethics alone. This nation asks for action, and action now.

Our greatest primary task is to put people to work. This is no unsolvable problem if we face it wisely and courageously. It can be accomplished in part by direct recruiting by the government itself, treating the task as we would treat the emergency of a war, but at the same time, through this employment, accomplishing greatly needed projects to stimulate and reorganize the use of our natural resources.

Hand in hand with this we must frankly recognize the overbalance of population in our industrial centers and, by engaging on a national scale in a redistribution, endeavor to provide a better use of the land for those best fitted for the land. The task can be helped by definite efforts to raise the values of agricultural products and with this the power to purchase the output of our cities. It can be helped by preventing realistically the tragedy of the growing loss through foreclosure of our small homes and our farms. It can be helped by insistence that the federal, state, and local governments act forthwith on the demand that their cost be drastically reduced. It can be helped by the unifying of relief activities which today are often scattered, uneconomical, and unequal. It can be helped by national planning for and supervision of all forms of transportation and of communications and other utilities which have a definitely public character. There are many ways in which it can be helped, but it can never be helped merely by talking about it. We must act and act quickly.

Finally, in our progress toward a resumption of work we require two safeguards against a return of the evils of the old order: there must be a strict supervision of all banking and credits and investments, so that there will be an end to speculation with other people's money; and there must be provision for an adequate but sound currency.

These are the lines of attack. I shall presently urge upon a new Congress, in special session, detailed measures for their fulfillment, and I shall seek the immediate assistance of the several States.

* * *

If I read the temper of our people correctly, we now realize as we have never realized before our interdependence on each other; that we cannot merely take but we must give as well; that if we are to go forward, we must move as a trained and loyal army willing to sacrifice for the good of a common discipline, because without such discipline no progress is made, no leadership becomes effective. We are, I know, ready and willing to submit our lives and property to such discipline, because it makes possible a leadership which aims at a larger good. This I propose to offer, pledging that the larger purposes will bind upon us all as a sacred obligation with a unity of duty hitherto evoked only in time of armed strife.

With this pledge taken, I assume unhesitatingly the leadership of this great army of our people dedicated to a disciplined attack upon our common problems.

Action in this image and to this end is feasible under the form of government which we have inherited from our ancestors. Our Constitution is so simple and practical that it is possible always to meet extraordinary needs by changes in emphasis and arrangement without loss of essential form. That is why our constitutional system has proved itself the most superbly enduring political mechanism the modern world has produced. It has met every stress of vast expansion of territory, of foreign wars, of bitter internal strife, of world relations.

It is to be hoped that the normal balance of executive and legislative authority may be wholly adequate to meet the unprecedented task before us. But it may be that an unprecedented demand and need for undelayed action may call for temporary departure from that normal balance of public procedure.

I am prepared under my constitutional duty to recommend the measures that a stricken nation in the midst of a stricken world may require. These measures, or such other measures as the Congress may build out of its experience and wisdom, I shall seek, within my constitutional authority, to bring to speedy adoption.

But in the event that the Congress shall fail to take one of these two courses, and in the event that the national emergency is still critical, I shall not evade the clear course of duty that will then confront me. I shall ask the Congress for the one remaining instrument to meet the crisis—broad Executive power to wage a war against the emergency, as great as the power that would be given to me if we were in fact invaded by a foreign foe.

For the trust reposed in me I will return the courage and the devotion that befit the time. I can do no less.

We face the arduous days that lie before us in the warm courage of national unity; with the clear consciousness of seeking old and precious moral values; with the clean satisfaction that comes from the stern performance of duty by old and young alike. We aim at the assurance of a rounded and permanent national life.

We do not distrust the future of essential democracy. The people of the United States have not failed. In their need they have registered a mandate that they want direct, vigorous action. They have asked for discipline and direction under leadership. They have made me the present instrument of their wishes. In the spirit of the gift I take it.

In this dedication of a nation, we humbly ask the blessing of God. May He protect each and every one of us. May He guide me in the days to come.

FIRST "FIRESIDE CHAT"

March 12, 1933

Immediately on taking office, Roosevelt tackled the banking crisis, which threatened a disastrous collapse of the nation's financial system. His aim was to assuage fears and restore confidence. This he did, unraveling complex financial ideas simply and without condescension. Masterful in his use of radio to connect with the people, Roosevelt spoke with a clarity and warmth that suggested an intimate tie to ordinary people. This skill served him well throughout his presidency.

I want to talk for a few minutes with the people of the United States about banking—with the comparatively few who understand the mechanics of banking but more particularly with the overwhelming majority who use banks for the making of deposits and the drawing of checks. I want to tell you what has been done in the last few days, why it was done, and what the next steps are going to be. I recognize that the many proclamations from state capitols and from Washington, the legislation, the Treasury regulations, etc., couched for the most part in banking and legal terms, should be explained for the benefit of the average citizen. I owe this in particular because of the fortitude and good temper with which everybody has accepted the inconvenience and hardships of the banking holiday. I know that when you understand what we in Washington have been about I shall continue to have your cooperation as fully as I have had your sympathy and help during the past week.

First of all, let me state the simple fact that when you deposit money in a bank the bank does not put the money into a safe deposit vault. It invests your money in many different forms of credit—bonds, commercial paper, mortgages and many other kinds of loans. In other words, the bank puts your money to work to keep the wheels of industry and of agriculture turning around. A comparatively small part of the money you put into the bank is kept in currency—an amount which in normal times is wholly sufficient to cover the cash needs of the average citizen. In other words, the total amount of all the currency in the country is only a small fraction of the total deposits in all of the banks.

What, then, happened during the last few days of February and the first few days of March? Because of undermined confidence on the part of the public, there was a general rush by a large portion of our population to turn bank deposits into currency or gold—a rush so great that the soundest banks could not get enough currency to meet the demand. The reason for this was that on the spur of the moment it was, of course, impossible to sell perfectly sound assets of a bank and convert them into cash except at panic prices far below their real value.

By the afternoon of March 3d, scarcely a bank in the country was open to do business. Proclamations temporarily closing them in whole or in part had been issued by the governors in almost all the States.

It was then that I issued the proclamation providing for the nation-wide bank holiday, and this was the first step in the government's reconstruction of our financial and economic fabric.

The second step was the legislation promptly and patriotically passed by the Congress confirming my proclamation and broadening my powers so that it became possible in view of the requirement of time to extend the holiday and lift the ban of that holiday gradually. This law also gave authority to develop a program of rehabilitation of our banking facilities. I want to tell our citizens in every part of the nation that the national Congress—Republicans and Democrats alike—showed by this action a devotion to public welfare and a realization of the emergency and the necessity for speed that it is difficult to match in our history.

The third stage has been the series of regulations permitting the banks to continue their functions to take care of the distribution of food and household necessities and the payment of payrolls.

This bank holiday, while resulting in many cases in great inconvenience, is affording us the opportunity to supply the currency necessary to meet the situation. No sound bank is a dollar worse off than it was when it closed its doors last Monday. Neither is any bank which may turn out not to be in a position for immediate opening. The new law allows the twelve Federal Reserve Banks to issue additional currency on good assets and thus the banks which reopen will be able to meet every legitimate call. The new currency is being sent out by the Bureau of Engraving and Printing in large volume to every part of the country. It is sound currency because it is backed by actual, good assets.

A question you will ask is this: why are all the banks not to be reopened at the same time? The answer is simple. Your government does not intend that the history of the past few years shall be repeated. We do not want and will not have another epidemic of bank failures.

As a result, we start tomorrow, Monday, with the opening of banks in the twelve Federal Reserve Bank cities—those banks which on first examination by the Treasury have already been found to be all right. This will be followed on Tuesday by the resumption of all their functions by banks already found to be sound in cities where there are recognized clearing houses. That means about 250 cities of the United States.

On Wednesday and succeeding days banks in smaller places all through the country will resume business, subject, of course, to the government's physical ability to complete its survey. It is necessary that the reopening of banks be extended over a period in order to permit the banks to make applications for necessary loans, to obtain currency needed to meet their requirements and to enable the government to make common sense checkups.

Let me make it clear to you that if your bank does not open the first day you are by no means justified in believing that it will not open. A bank that opens on one of the subsequent days is in exactly the same status as the bank that opens tomorrow.

I know that many people are worrying about state banks not members of the Federal Reserve System. These banks can and will receive assistance from member banks and from the Reconstruction Finance Corporation. These state banks are following the same course as the national banks except that they get their licenses to resume business from the state authorities, and these authorities have been asked by the Secretary of the Treasury to permit their good banks to open up on the same schedule as the national banks. I am confident that the state banking departments will be as careful as the national government in the policy relating to the opening of banks and will follow the same broad policy.

It is possible that when the banks resume a very few people who have not recovered from their fear may again begin withdrawals. Let me make it clear that the banks will take care of all needs—and it is my belief that hoarding during the past week has become an exceedingly unfashionable pastime. It needs no prophet to tell you that when the people find that they can get their money—that they can get it when they want it for all legitimate purposes—the phantom of fear will soon be laid. People will again be glad to have their money where it will be safely taken care of and where they can use it conveniently at any time. I can assure you that it is safer to keep your money in a reopened bank than under the mattress.

The success of our whole great national program depends, of course, upon the cooperation of the public—on its intelligent support and use of a reliable system.

Remember that the essential accomplishment of the new legislation is that it makes it possible for banks more readily to convert their assets into cash than was the case before. More liberal provision has been made for banks to borrow on these assets at the Reserve Banks and more liberal provision has also been made for issuing currency on the security of these good assets. This currency is not fiat currency. It is issued only on adequate security, and every good bank has an abundance of such security.

One more point before I close. There will be, of course, some banks unable to reopen without being reorganized. The new law allows the government to assist in making these reorganizations quickly and effectively and even allows the government to subscribe to at least a part of new capital which may be required.

I hope you can see from this elemental recital of what your government is doing that there is nothing complex, or radical, in the process.

We had a bad banking situation. Some of our bankers had shown themselves either incompetent or dishonest in their handling of the people's funds. They had used the money entrusted to them in speculations and unwise loans. This was, of course, not true in the vast majority of our banks, but it was true in enough of them to shock the people for a time into a sense of insecurity and to put them into a frame of mind where they did not differentiate, but seemed to assume that the acts of a comparative few had tainted them all. It was the government's job to straighten out this situation and do it as quickly as possible. And the job is being performed.

I do not promise you that every bank will be reopened or that individual losses will not be suffered, but there will be no losses that possibly could be avoided; and there would have been more and greater losses had we continued to drift. I can even promise you salvation for some at least of the sorely pressed banks. We shall be engaged not merely in reopening sound banks but in the creation of sound banks through reorganization.

It has been wonderful to me to catch the note of confidence from all over the country. I can never be sufficiently grateful to the people for the loyal support they have given me in their acceptance of the judgment that has dictated our course, even though all our processes may not have seemed clear to them.

After all, there is an element in the readjustment of our financial system more important than currency, more important than gold, and that is the confidence of the people. Confidence and courage are the essentials of success in carrying out our plan. You people must have faith; you must not be stampeded by rumors or guesses. Let us unite in banishing fear. We have provided the machinery to restore our financial system; it is up to you to support and make it work.

It is your problem no less than it is mine. Together we cannot fail.

ADMINISTRATION OBJECTIVES MESSAGE TO THE CONGRESS

June 8, 1934

At a time when authoritarian regimes were overtaking recently established democracies, Roosevelt affirmed the ability of American democracy to endure in times of crisis. The president focused on the objectives of the work in progress: decent shelter, productive work, and a measure of security. These he described as matters of right, and to secure these rights in modern times required the action of government as well as private initiative. The message served to broadcast the values of his administration and to forecast legislation to come.

To the Congress:

You are completing a work begun in March 1933, which will be regarded for a long time as a splendid justification of the vitality of representative government. I greet you and express once more my appreciation of the cooperation which has proved so effective. Only a small number of the items of our program remain to be enacted and I am confident that you will pass on them before adjournment. Many other pending measures are sound in conception, but must, for lack of time or of adequate information, be deferred to the session of the next Congress. In the meantime, we can well seek to adjust many of these measures into certain larger plans of governmental policy for the future of the nation.

You and I, as the responsible directors of these policies and actions, may, with good reason, look to the future with confidence, just as we may look to the past fifteen months with reasonable satisfaction.

On the side of relief we have extended material aid to millions of our fellow citizens.

On the side of recovery, we have helped to lift agriculture and industry from a condition of utter prostration.

But, in addition to these immediate tasks of relief and recovery, we have properly, necessarily and with overwhelming approval determined to safeguard these tasks by rebuilding many of the structures of our economic life and of reorganizing it in order to prevent a recurrence of collapse.

It is childish to speak of recovery first and reconstruction afterward. In the very nature of the processes of recovery, we must avoid the destructive influences of the past. We have shown the world that democracy has within it the elements necessary to its own salvation.

Less hopeful countries where the ways of democracy are very new may revert to the autocracy of yesterday. The American people can be trusted to decide wisely upon the measures taken by the government to eliminate the abuses of the past and to proceed in the direction of the greater good for the greater number. . . .

Among our objectives, I place the security of the men, women and children of the nation first.

This security for the individual and for the family concerns itself primarily with three factors. People want decent homes to live in; they want to locate them where they can engage in productive work; and they want some safeguard against misfortunes which cannot be wholly eliminated in this man-made world of ours.

In a simple and primitive civilization, homes were to be had for the building. The bounties of nature in a new land provided crude but adequate food and shelter. When land failed, our ancestors moved on to better land. It was always possible to push back the frontier, but the frontier has now disappeared. Our task involves the making of a better living out of the lands that we have.

So, also, security was attained in the earlier days through the interdependence of members of families upon each other and of the families within a small community upon each other. The complexities of great communities and of organized industry make less real these simple means of security. Therefore, we are compelled to employ the active interest of the nation as a whole through government in order to encourage a greater security for each individual who composes it.

With the full cooperation of the Congress we have already made a serious attack upon the problem of housing in our great cities. Millions of dollars have been appropriated for housing projects by federal and local authorities, often with the generous assistance of private owners. The task thus begun must be pursued for many years to come. There is ample private money for sound housing projects; and the Congress, in a measure now before you, can stimulate the lending of money for the modernization of existing homes and the building of new homes. In pursuing this policy we are working toward the ultimate objective of making it possible for American families to live as Americans should.

In regard to the second factor, economic circumstances and the forces of nature themselves dictate the need of constant thought as to the means by which a wise Government may help the necessary readjustment of the population. We cannot fail to act when hundreds of thousands of families live where there is no reasonable prospect of a living in the years to come. This is especially a national problem. Unlike most of the leading nations of the world, we have so far failed to create a national policy for the development of our land and water resources and for their better use by those people who cannot make a living in their present positions. Only thus can we permanently eliminate many millions of people from the relief rolls on which their names are now found.

* * *

The third factor relates to security against the hazards and vicissitudes of life. Fear and worry based on unknown danger contribute to social unrest and economic demoralization If, as our Constitution tells us, our federal government was established among other things "to promote the general welfare," it is our plain duty to provide for that security upon which welfare depends.

Next winter we may well undertake the great task of furthering the security of the citizen and his family through social insurance.

This is not an untried experiment. Lessons of experience are available from states, from industries and from many nations of the civilized world. The various types of social insurance are interrelated; and I think it is difficult to attempt to solve them piecemeal. Hence, I am looking for a sound means which I can recommend to provide at once security against several of the great disturbing factors in life— especially those which relate to unemployment and old age. I believe there should be a maximum of cooperation between states and the federal government. I believe that the funds necessary to provide this insurance should be raised by contribution rather than by an increase in general taxation. Above all, I am convinced that social insurance should be national in scope, although the several states should meet at least a large portion of the cost of management, leaving to the federal government the responsibility of investing, maintaining, and safeguarding the funds constituting the necessary insurance reserves. . . .

These three great objectives—the security of the home, the security of livelihood, and the security of social insurance—are, it seems to me, a minimum of the promise that we can offer to the American people. They constitute a right which belongs to every individual and every family willing to work. They are the essential fulfillment of measures already taken toward relief, recovery, and reconstruction.

This seeking for a greater measure of welfare and happiness does not indicate a change in values. It is rather a return to values lost in the course of our economic development and expansion.

Ample scope is left for the exercise of private initiative. In fact, in the process of recovery, I am greatly hoping that repeated promises of private investment and private initiative to relieve the government in the immediate future of much of the burden it has assumed, will be fulfilled. We have not imposed undue restrictions upon business. We have not opposed the incentive of reasonable and legitimate private profit. We have sought rather to enable certain aspects of business to regain the confidence of the public. We have sought to put forward the rule of fair play in finance and industry.

It is true that there are a few among us who would still go back. These few offer no substitute for the gains already made, nor any hope for making future gains for human happiness. They loudly assert that individual liberty is being restricted by government, but when they are asked what individual liberties they have lost, they are put to it to answer.

We must dedicate ourselves anew to a recovery of the old and sacred possessive rights for which mankind has constantly struggled—homes, livelihood, and individual security. The road to these values is the way of progress. Neither you nor I will rest content until we have done our utmost to move further on that road.

FIRESIDE CHAT ON THE NRA

September 30, 1934

The president reached beyond the pundits directly to the people in this fireside chat to review administration actions and to focus on his hopes for the National Recovery Administration (NRA). In clear language, he untangled the complexities of NRA functions aimed at cooling labor-management industrial strife and increasing production. Roosevelt conceded the possibility that adjustment and correctives might be necessary, displaying a human dimension that resonated with his listeners.

Three months have passed since I talked with you shortly after the adjournment of the Congress. Tonight I continue that report, though, because of the shortness of time, I must defer a number of subjects to a later date. Recently the most notable public questions that have concerned us all have had to do with industry and labor and with respect to these, certain developments have taken place which I consider of importance. I am happy to report that after years of uncertainty, culminating in the collapse of the spring of 1933, we are bringing order out of the old chaos with a greater certainty of the employment of labor at a reasonable wage and of more business at a fair profit. These governmental and industrial developments hold promise of new achievements for the nation. . . .

Our first problem was, of course, the banking situation because, as you know, the banks had collapsed. Some banks could not be saved but the great majority of them, either through their own resources or with Government aid, have been restored to complete public confidence. This has given safety to millions of depositors in these banks. Closely following this great constructive effort we have, through various federal agencies, saved debtors and creditors alike in many other fields of enterprise such as loans on farm mortgages and home mortgages; loans to the railroads and insurance companies and, finally, help for home owners and industry itself.

In all of these efforts, the Government has come to the assistance of business and with the full expectation that the money used to assist these enterprises will eventually be repaid. I believe it will be.

The second step we have taken in the restoration of normal business enterprise has been to clean up thoroughly unwholesome conditions in the field of investment. In this, we have had assistance from many bankers and business men, most of whom recognize the past evils in the banking system, in the sale of securities, in the deliberate encouragement of stock gambling, in the sale of unsound mortgages and in many other ways in which the public lost billions of dollars. They saw that without changes in the policies and methods of investment there could be no recovery of public confidence in the security of savings. The country now enjoys the safety of bank savings under the new banking laws, the careful checking of new securities under the Securities Act and the curtailment of rank stock speculation through the Securities Exchange Act. I sincerely hope that as a result people will be discouraged in unhappy efforts to get rich quick by speculating in securities. The average person almost always loses. Only a very small minority of the people of this country believe in gambling as a substitute for the old philosophy of Benjamin Franklin that the way to wealth is through work.

In meeting the problems of industrial recovery, the chief agency of the government has been the National Recovery Administration. Under its guidance, trades and industries covering over 90 percent of all industrial employees have adopted codes of fair competition, which have been approved by the President. Under these codes, in the industries covered, child labor has been eliminated. The work day and the work week have been shortened. Minimum wages have been established and other wages adjusted toward a rising standard of living. The emergency purpose of the NRA was to put men to work and since its creation, more than four million persons have been reemployed, in great part through the cooperation of American business brought about under the codes.

Benefits of the Industrial Recovery Program have come not only to labor in the form of new jobs, in relief from overwork and in relief from underpay, but also to the owners and managers of industry because, together with a great increase in the payrolls, there has come a substantial rise in the total of industrial profits—a rise from a deficit figure in the first quarter of 1933 at a level of sustained profits within one year from the inauguration of NRA.

Now, it should not be expected that even employed labor and capital would be completely satisfied with present conditions. Employed workers have not by any means all enjoyed a return to the earnings of prosperous times, although millions of hitherto underprivileged workers are today far better paid than ever before. Also, billions of dollars of invested capital have today a greater security of present and future earning power than before. This is because of the establishment of fair, competitive standards and because of relief from unfair competition in wage cutting which depresses markets and destroys purchasing power. But it is an undeniable fact that the restoration of other billions of sound investments to a reasonable earning power could not be brought about in one year. There is no magic formula, no economic panacea, which could simply revive overnight the heavy industries and the trades dependent upon them.

* * *

Let me call your attention to the fact that the National Industrial Recovery Act gave business men the opportunity they had sought for years to improve business conditions through what has been called self-government in industry. If the codes which have been written have been too complicated, if they have gone too far in such matters as price fixing and limitation of production, let it be remembered that so far as possible, consistent with the immediate public interest of this past year and the vital necessity of improving labor conditions, the representatives of trade industry were permitted to write their ideas into the codes. It is now time to review these actions as a whole to determine through deliberative means in the light of experience, from the standpoint of the good of the industries themselves, as well as the general public interest, whether the methods and policies adopted in the emergency have been best calculated to promote industrial recovery and a permanent improvement of business and labor conditions. There may be a serious question as to the wisdom of many of those devices to control production, or to prevent destructive price cutting which many business organizations have insisted were necessary, or whether their effect may have been to prevent that volume of production which would make possible lower prices and increased employment. Another question arises as to whether in fixing minimum wages on the basis of an hourly or weekly wage we have reached into the heart of the problem, which is to provide such annual earnings for the lowest paid worker as will meet his minimum needs. We also question the wisdom of extending code requirements suited to the great industrial centers and to large employers, to the great number of small employers in the smaller communities.

During the last twelve months, our industrial recovery has been to some extent retarded by strikes, including a few of major importance. I would not minimize the inevitable losses to employers and employees and to the general public through such conflicts. But I would point out that the extent and severity of labor disputes during this period have been far less than in any previous comparable period.

When the business men of the country were demanding the right to organize themselves adequately to promote their legitimate interests; when the farmers were demanding legislation which would give them opportunities and incentives to organize themselves for a common advance, it was natural that the workers should seek and obtain a statutory declaration of their constitutional right to organize themselves for collective bargaining embodied in Section 7-A of the National Industrial Recovery Act.

Machinery set up by the federal government has provided some new methods of adjustment. Both employers and employees must share the blame of not using them as fully as they should. . . .

It is time that we made a clean-cut effort to bring about that united action of management and labor, which is one of the high purposes of the Recovery Act. We have passed through more than a year of education. Step by step, we have created all the government agencies necessary to insure, as a general rule, industrial peace, with justice for all those willing to use these agencies whenever their voluntary bargaining fails to produce a necessary agreement.

There should be at least a full and fair trial given to these means of ending industrial warfare; and in such an effort we should be able to secure for employers and employees and consumers the benefits that all derive from the continuous, peaceful operation of our essential enterprises.

Accordingly, I propose to confer within the coming month with small groups of those truly representative of large employers of labor and of large groups of organized labor, in order to seek their cooperation in establishing what I may describe as a specific trial period of industrial peace. . . .

Closely allied to the NRA is the program of public works provided for in the same Act and designed to put more men back to work, both directly on the public works themselves, and indirectly in the industries supplying the materials for these public works. To those who say that our expenditures for public works and other means for recovery are a waste that we cannot afford I answer that no country, however rich, can afford the waste of its human resources. Demoralization caused by vast unemployment is our greatest extravagance. Morally, it is the greatest menace to our social order. Some people try to tell me that we must make up our minds that for the future we shall permanently have millions of unemployed just as other countries have had them for over a decade. What may be necessary for those countries is not my responsibility to determine. But as for this country, I stand or fall by my refusal to accept as a necessary condition of our future a permanent army of unemployed. On the contrary, we must make it a national principle that we will not tolerate a large army of unemployed and that we will arrange our national economy to end our present unemployment as soon as we can and then to take wise measures against its return. I do not want to think that it is the destiny of any American to remain permanently on relief rolls. . . .

Nearly all Americans are sensible and calm people. We do not get greatly excited nor is our peace of mind disturbed, whether we be businessmen or workers or farmers, by awesome pronouncements concerning the unconstitutionality of some of our measures of recovery and relief and reform. We are not frightened by reactionary lawyers or political editors. All of these cries have been heard before. . . .

In our efforts for recovery, we have avoided, on the one hand, the theory that business should and must be taken over into an all-embracing government. We have avoided, on the other hand, the equally untenable theory that it is an interference with liberty to offer reasonable help when private enterprise is in need of help. The course we have followed fits the American practice of Government, a practice of taking action step by step, of regulating only to meet concrete needs, a practice of courageous recognition of change. I believe with Abraham Lincoln, that "The legitimate object of government is to do for a community of people whatever they need to have done but cannot do at all or cannot do so well for themselves in their separate and individual capacities."

I am not for a return to that definition of liberty under which for many years a free people were being gradually regimented into the service of the privileged few. I prefer and I am sure you prefer that broader definition of liberty under which we are moving forward to greater freedom, to greater security for the average man than he has ever known before in the history of America.

ANNUAL MESSAGE TO THE CONGRESS

January 4, 1935

After nearly two years in office, Roosevelt's annual message referred to the "new economic order" his administration had established. It was necessary, he argued, to combine recovery with reform in order to treat the causes as well as the symptoms of the nation's malaise. His aim was not to attack the profit motive but to confront the excesses of capitalist greed and power. He firmly rejected the idea of perpetual relief, which damaged the human spirit, but insisted on the obligation of government to assure security for the people.

The Constitution wisely provides that the Chief Executive shall report to the Congress on the state of the Union, for through you, the chosen legislative representatives, our citizens everywhere may fairly judge the progress of our governing. I am confident that today, in the light of the events of the past two years, you do not consider it merely a trite phrase when I tell you that I am truly glad to greet you and that I look forward to common counsel, to useful cooperation, and to genuine friendships between us. . . .

As the various parts in the program begun in the Extraordinary Session of the 73rd Congress shape themselves in practical administration, the unity of our program reveals itself to the nation. The outlines of the new economic order, rising from the disintegration of the old, are apparent. We test what we have done as our measures take root in the living texture of life. We see where we have built wisely and where we can do still better.

The attempt to make a distinction between recovery and reform is a narrowly conceived effort to substitute the appearance of reality for reality itself. When a man is convalescing from illness, wisdom dictates not only cure of the symptoms, but also removal of their cause.

It is important to recognize that while we seek to outlaw specific abuses, the American objective of today has an infinitely deeper, finer and more lasting purpose than mere repression. Thinking people in almost every country of the world have come to realize certain fundamental difficulties with which civilization must reckon. Rapid changes—the machine age, the advent of universal and rapid communication and many other new factors—have brought new problems. Succeeding generations have attempted to keep pace by reforming in piecemeal fashion this or that attendant abuse. As a result, evils overlap and reform becomes confused and frustrated. We lose sight, from time to time, of our ultimate human objectives.

Let us, for a moment, strip from our simple purpose the confusion that results from a multiplicity of detail and from millions of written and spoken words.

We find our population suffering from old inequalities, little changed by past sporadic remedies. In spite of our efforts and in spite of our talk, we have not weeded out the overprivileged, and we have not effectively lifted up the underprivileged. Both of these manifestations of injustice have retarded happiness. No wise man has any intention of destroying what is known as the profit motive; because by the profit motive we mean the right by work to earn a decent livelihood for ourselves and for our families.

We have, however, a clear mandate from the people, that Americans must forswear that conception of the acquisition of wealth which, through excessive profits, creates undue private power over private affairs and, to our misfortune, over public affairs as well. In building toward this end, we do not destroy ambition, nor do we seek to divide our wealth into equal shares on stated occasions. We continue to recognize the greater ability of some to earn more than others. But we do assert that the ambition of the individual to obtain for him and his a proper security, a reasonable leisure, and a decent living throughout life, is an ambition to be preferred to the appetite for great wealth and great power.

I recall to your attention my message to the Congress last June in which I said: "Among our objectives I place the security of the men, women and children of the nation first." That remains our first and continuing task; and in a very real sense every major legislative enactment of this Congress should be a component part of it.

In defining immediate factors which enter into our quest, I have spoken to the Congress and the people of three great divisions:

1. The security of a livelihood through the better use of the national resources of the land in which we live.
2. The security against the major hazards and vicissitudes of life.
3. The security of decent homes.

I am now ready to submit to the Congress a broad program designed ultimately to establish all three of these factors of security—a program which, because of many lost years, will take many future years to fulfill.

A study of our national resources, more comprehensive than any previously made, shows the vast amount of necessary and practicable work which needs to be done for the development and preservation of our natural wealth for the enjoyment and advantage of our people in generations to come. The sound use of land and water is far more comprehensive than the mere planting of trees, building of dams, distributing of electricity or retirement of sub-marginal land. It recognizes that stranded populations, either in the country or the city, cannot have security under the conditions that now surround them.

To this end, we are ready to begin to meet this problem—the intelligent care of population throughout our nation, in accordance with an intelligent distribution of the means of livelihood for that population. A definite program for putting people to work, of which I shall speak in a moment, is a component part of this greater program of security of livelihood through the better use of our national resources.

Closely related to the broad problem of livelihood is that of security against the major hazards of life. Here also, a comprehensive survey of what has been attempted or accomplished in many nations and in many states proves to me that the time has come for action by the national government. I shall send to you, in a few days, definite recommendations based on these studies. These recommendations will cover the broad subjects of unemployment insurance and old age insurance, of benefits for children, for mothers, for the handicapped, for maternity care and for other aspects of dependency and illness where a beginning can now be made.

The third factor—better homes for our people—has also been the subject of experimentation and study. Here, too, the first practical steps can be made through the proposals which I shall suggest in relation to giving work to the unemployed.

Whatever we plan and whatever we do should be in the light of these three clear objectives of security.

* * *

But the stark fact before us is that great numbers still remain unemployed.

A large proportion of these unemployed and their dependents have been forced on the relief rolls. The burden on the federal government has grown with great rapidity. We have here a human as well as an economic problem. When humane considerations are concerned,

Americans give them precedence. The lessons of history, confirmed by the evidence immediately before me, show conclusively that continued dependence upon relief induces a spiritual and moral disintegration fundamentally destructive to the national fiber. To dole out relief in this way is to administer a narcotic, a subtle destroyer of the human spirit. It is inimical to the dictates of sound policy. It is in violation of the traditions of America. Work must be found for able-bodied but destitute workers.

The federal government must and shall quit this business of relief.

I am not willing that the vitality of our people be further sapped by the giving of cash, of market baskets, of a few hours of weekly work cutting grass, raking leaves or picking up papers in the public parks. We must preserve not only the bodies of the unemployed from destitution but also their self-respect, their self-reliance and courage and determination. This decision brings me to the problem of what the government should do with approximately 5 million unemployed now on the relief rolls.

About one million and a half of these belong to the group which in the past was dependent upon local welfare efforts. Most of them are unable for one reason or another to maintain themselves independently—for the most part, through no fault of their own. Such people, in the days before the Great Depression, were cared for by local efforts—by states, by counties, by towns, by cities, by churches and by private welfare agencies. It is my thought that in the future they must be cared for as they were before. I stand ready through my own personal efforts, and through the public influence of the office that I hold, to help these local agencies to get the means necessary to assume this burden.

The security legislation which I shall propose to the Congress will, I am confident, be of assistance to local effort in the care of this type of cases. Local responsibility can and will be resumed, for, after all, common sense tells us that the wealth necessary for this task existed and still exists in the local community, and the dictates of sound administration require that this responsibility be in the first instance a local one.

There are, however, an additional three and one half million employable people who are on relief. With them the problem is different and the responsibility is different. This group was the victim of a nation-wide depression caused by conditions which were not local but national. The federal government is the only governmental agency with sufficient power and credit to meet this situation. We have assumed this task and we shall not shrink from it in the future. It is a duty dictated by every intelligent consideration of national policy to ask you to make it possible for the United States to give employment to all of these three and one half million employable people now on relief, pending their absorption in a rising tide of private employment.

It is my thought that with the exception of certain of the normal public building operations of the government, all emergency public works shall be united in a single new and greatly enlarged plan.

With the establishment of this new system, we can supersede the Federal Emergency Relief Administration with a coordinated authority which will be charged with the orderly liquidation of our present relief activities and the substitution of a national chart for the giving of work.

This new program of emergency public employment should be governed by a number of practical principles.

1. All work undertaken should be useful—not just for a day, or a year, but useful in the sense that it affords permanent improvement in living conditions or that it creates future new wealth for the nation.
2. Compensation on emergency public projects should be in the form of security payments which should be larger than the amount now received as a relief dole, but at the same time not so large as to encourage the rejection of opportunities for private employment or the leaving of private employment to engage in government work.
3. Projects should be undertaken on which a large percentage of direct labor can be used.
4. Preference should be given to those projects which will be self-liquidating in the sense that there is a reasonable expectation that the government will get its money back at some future time.
5. The projects undertaken should be selected and planned so as to compete as little as possible with private enterprises. This suggests that if it were not for the necessity of giving useful work to the unemployed now on relief, these projects in most instances would not now be undertaken.
6. The planning of projects would seek to assure work during the coming fiscal year to the individuals now on relief, or until such time as private employment is available. In order to make adjustment to increasing private employment, work should be planned with a view to tapering it off in proportion to the speed with which the emergency workers are offered positions with private employers.

7. Effort should be made to locate projects where they will serve the greatest unemployment needs as shown by present relief rolls, and the broad program of the National Resources Board should be freely used for guidance in selection. Our ultimate objective being the enrichment of human lives, the government has the primary duty to use its emergency expenditures as much as possible to serve those who cannot secure the advantages of private capital.

* * *

The ledger of the past year shows many more gains than losses. Let us not forget that, in addition to saving millions from utter destitution, child labor has been for the moment outlawed, thousands of homes saved to their owners and most important of all, the morale of the nation has been restored. Viewing the year 1934 as a whole, you and I can agree that we have a generous measure of reasons for giving thanks.

It is not empty optimism that moves me to a strong hope in the coming year. We can, if we will, make 1935 a genuine period of good feeling, sustained by a sense of purposeful progress. Beyond the material recovery, I sense a spiritual recovery as well. The people of America are turning as never before to those permanent values that are not limited to the physical objectives of life. There are growing signs of this on every hand. In the face of these spiritual impulses, we are sensible of the Divine Providence to which nations turn now, as always, for guidance and fostering care.

ACCEPTING RENOMINATION

Philadelphia, June 27, 1936

Accepting his party's nomination for a second term, Roosevelt told Americans they had a "rendezvous with destiny," an enduring phrase with which he and his administration would be frequently identified. "Economic royalists" was another phrase here that served well in his repeated critiques of those who abused the power of capital to create a new kind of aristocracy. His speech set the fighting tone for the campaign to fend off the bitter attacks leveled at him and his New Deal. He struck a recurring theme in his political outlook: real freedom required a measure of economic well-being. His invocation of faith, hope, and charity was consistent with frequent association of the work of social and economic reform with his religious values.

Here, and in every community throughout the land, we are met at a time of great moment to the future of the nation. It is an occasion to be dedicated to the simple and sincere expression of an attitude toward problems, the determination of which will profoundly affect America.

* * *

Philadelphia is a good city in which to write American history. This is fitting ground on which to reaffirm the faith of our fathers; to pledge ourselves to restore to the people a wider freedom; to give to 1936 as the founders gave to 1776—an American way of life.

That very word freedom, in itself and of necessity, suggests freedom from some restraining power. In 1776, we sought freedom from the tyranny of a political autocracy—from the 18th-century royalists who held special privileges from the crown. It was to perpetuate their privilege that they governed without the consent of the governed; that they denied the right of free assembly and free speech; that they restricted the worship of God; that they put the average man's property and the average man's life in pawn to the mercenaries of dynastic power; that they regimented the people.

And so, it was to win freedom from the tyranny of political autocracy that the American Revolution was fought. That victory gave the business of governing into the hands of the average man, who won the right with his neighbors to make and order his own destiny through his own government. Political tyranny was wiped out at Philadelphia on July 4, 1776.

Since that struggle, however, man's inventive genius released new forces in our land which reordered the lives of our people. The age of machinery, of railroads, of steam and electricity, the telegraph and the radio, mass production, mass distribution—all of these combined to bring forward a new civilization and with it a new problem for those who sought to remain free.

For out of this modern civilization economic royalists carved new dynasties. New kingdoms were built upon concentration of control over material things. Through new uses of corporations, banks and securities, new machinery of industry and agriculture, of labor and capital—all undreamed of by the fathers—the whole structure of modern life was impressed into this royal service.

There was no place among this royalty for our many thousands of small business men and merchants who sought to make worthy use of the American system of initiative and profit. They were no more free than the worker or the farmer. Even honest and progressive-minded men of wealth, aware of their obligations to their generation, could never know just where they fitted into this dynastic scheme of things.

It was natural and perhaps human that the privileged princes of these new economic dynasties, thirsting for power, reached out for control over government itself. They created a new despotism and wrapped it in the robes of legal sanction. In its service new mercenaries sought to regiment the people, their labor, their property. And as a result the average man once more confronts the problem that faced the Minute Man.

The hours men and women worked, the wages they received, the conditions of their labor—these had passed beyond the control of the people, and were imposed by this new industrial dictatorship. The savings of the average family, the capital of the small business man, the investments set aside for old age—other people's money— these were tools which the new economic royalty used to dig itself in.

Those who tilled the soil no longer reaped the rewards which were their right. The small measure of their gains was decreed by men in distant cities.

Throughout the nation, opportunity was limited by monopoly. Individual initiative was crushed in the cogs of a great machine. The field open for free business was more and more restricted. Private enterprise, indeed, became too private. It became privileged enterprise, not free enterprise.

An old English judge once said: "Necessitous men are not free men." Liberty requires opportunity to make a living—a living decent according to the standard of the time, a living which gives man not only enough to live by, but something to live for.

For too many of us the political equality we once had won was meaningless in the face of economic inequality. A small group had concentrated into their own hands an almost complete control over other people's property, other people's money, other people's labor—other people's lives. For too many of us life was no longer free; liberty no longer real; men could no longer follow the pursuit of happiness.

Against economic tyranny such as this, the American citizen could appeal only to the organized power of government. The collapse of 1929 showed up the despotism for what it was. The election of 1932 was the people's mandate to end it. Under that mandate it is being ended.

The royalists of the economic order have conceded that political freedom was the business of the Government, but they have maintained that economic slavery was nobody's business. They granted that the government could protect the citizen in his right to vote, but they denied that the government could do anything to protect the citizen in his right to work and his right to live.

Today we stand committed to the proposition that freedom is no half-and-half affair. If the average citizen is guaranteed equal opportunity in the polling place, he must have equal opportunity in the market place.

These economic royalists complain that we seek to overthrow the institutions of America. What they really complain of is that we seek to take away their power. Our allegiance to American institutions requires the overthrow of this kind of power. In vain they seek to hide behind the flag and the Constitution. In their blindness, they forget what the flag and the Constitution stand for. Now, as always, they stand for democracy, not tyranny; for freedom, not subjection; and against a dictatorship by mob rule and the over privileged alike. . . .

The defeats and victories of these years have given to us as a people a new understanding of our government and of ourselves. Never since the early days of the New England town meeting have the affairs of government been so widely discussed and so clearly appreciated. It has been brought home to us that the only effective guide for the safety of this most worldly of worlds, the greatest guide of all, is moral principle.

We do not see faith, hope and charity as unattainable ideals, but we use them as stout supports of a nation fighting the fight for freedom in a modern civilization.

Faith—in the soundness of democracy in the midst of dictatorships.

Hope—renewed because we know so well the progress we have made.

Charity—in the true spirit of that grand old word. For charity literally translated from the original means love, the love that understands, that does not merely share the wealth of the giver, but in true sympathy and wisdom helps men to help themselves.

We seek not merely to make government a mechanical implement, but to give it the vibrant personal character that is the very embodiment of human charity.

We are poor indeed, if this nation cannot afford to lift from every recess of American life the dread fear of the unemployed that they are not needed in the world. We cannot afford to accumulate a deficit in the books of human fortitude.

In the place of the palace of privilege, we seek to build a temple out of faith and hope and charity.

It is a sobering thing, my friends, to be a servant of this great cause. We try in our daily work to remember that the cause belongs not to us, but to the people. The standard is not in the hands of you and me alone. It is carried by America. We seek daily to profit from experience, to learn to do better as our task proceeds.

Governments can err, presidents do make mistakes, but the immortal Dante tells us that divine justice weighs the sins of the cold-blooded and the sins of the warm-hearted in different scales.

Better the occasional faults of a government that lives in a spirit of charity than the consistent omissions of a government frozen in the ice of its own indifference.

There is a mysterious cycle in human events. To some generations much is given. Of other generations, much is expected. This generation of Americans has a rendezvous with destiny.

In this world of ours, in other lands, there are some people, who, in times past, have lived and fought for freedom, and seem to have grown too weary to carry on the fight. They have sold their heritage of freedom for the illusion of a living. They have yielded their democracy.

I believe in my heart that only our success can stir their ancient hope. They begin to know that here in America we are waging a great and successful war. It is not alone a war against want and destitution and economic demoralization. It is more than that—it is a war for the survival of democracy. We are fighting to save a great and precious form of government for ourselves and for the world.

I accept the commission you have tendered me. I join with you. I am enlisted for the duration of the war.

OPENING THE 1936 PRESIDENTIAL CAMPAIGN

Address to the Democratic State Convention, Syracuse, September 29, 1936

This was a frankly partisan speech for a partisan occasion. Roosevelt reminded his audience of the dangerous conditions in the depths of the Depression that might have led to the acceptance of radical options. He confronted the conservative charges ascribing radicalism and even Communism to his work. In what would be one of the themes of the campaign, he emphasized the need for reforms in order to preserve and defend traditional values; thus the image of the liberal as conservative.

"I am that kind of conservative because I am that kind of liberal."

Tonight you and I join forces for the 1936 campaign. We enter it with confidence. Never was there greater need for fidelity to the underlying conception of Americanism than there is today. And once again it is given to our party to carry the message of that Americanism to the people.

The task on our party is twofold: First, as simple patriotism requires, to separate the false from the real issues; and, secondly, with facts and without rancor, to clarify the real problems for the American public.

There will be—there are—many false issues. In that respect, this will be no different from other campaigns. Partisans, not willing to face realities, will drag out red herrings—as they have always done—to divert attention from the trail of their own weaknesses.

This practice is as old as our democracy. . . .

This year it is Russian. Desperate in mood, angry at failure, cunning in purpose, individuals and groups are seeking to make Communism an issue in an election where Communism is not a controversy between the two major parties.

Here and now, once and for all, let us bury that red herring and destroy that false issue. You are familiar with my background; you know my heritage; and you are familiar, especially in the State of New York, with my public service extending back over a quarter of a century. For nearly four years, I have been President of the United States. A long record has been written. In that record, both in this State and in the national capital, you will find a simple, clear, and consistent adherence not only to the letter, but to the spirit of the American form of government. . . .

There is no difference between the major parties as to what they think about Communism. But there is a very great difference between the two parties in what they do about Communism.

I must tell you why. Communism is a manifestation of the social unrest which always comes with widespread economic adjustment. We in the Democratic Party have not been content merely to denounce this menace. We have been realistic enough to face it. We have been intelligent enough to do something about it. And the world has seen the results of what we have done. In the spring of 1933, we faced a crisis which was the ugly fruit of 12 years of neglect of the causes of economic and social unrest. It was a crisis made to order for all those who would overthrow our form of government.

Do I need to recall to you the fear of those days—the reports of those who piled supplies in their basements, who laid plans to get their fortunes across the border, who got themselves hideaways in the country against the upending upheaval? Do I need to recall the law-abiding heads of peaceful families, who began to wonder, as they saw their children starve, how they would get the bread they saw in the bakery window? Do I need to recall the homeless boys who were traveling in bands through the countryside seeking work, seeking food—desperate because they could find neither? Do I need to recall the farmers who banded together with pitchforks to keep the sheriff from selling the farm home under foreclosure? Do I need to recall the powerful leaders of industry and banking who came to me in Washington in those early days of 1933 pleading to be saved?

Most people in the United States remember today the fact that starvation was averted, that homes and farms were saved, that banks were reopened, that crop prices rose, that industry revived, and that the dangerous forces subversive of our form of government were turned aside.

A few people—a few only—unwilling to remember, seem to have forgotten those days.

In the summer of 1933, a nice old gentleman wearing a silk hat fell off the end of a pier. He was unable to swim. A friend ran down the pier, dived overboard, and pulled him out; but the silk hat floated off with the tide. After the old gentleman had been revived, he was effusive in his thanks. He praised his friend for saving his life. Today, three years later, the old gentleman is berating his friend because the silk hat was lost.

Why did that crisis of 1929 to 1933 pass without disaster? The answer is found in the record of what we did. Early in the campaign of 1932,

I said, "To meet by reaction that danger of radicalism is to invite disaster. Reaction is no barrier to the radical, it is a challenge, a provocation. The way to meet that danger is to offer a workable program of reconstruction, and the party to offer it is the party with clean hands." We met the emergency with emergency action. But far more important than that we went to the roots of the problem, and attacked the cause of the crisis. We were against revolution. Therefore, we waged war against those conditions which make revolutions—against the inequalities and resentments which breed them. In America in 1933, the people did not attempt to remedy wrongs by overthrowing their institutions. Americans were made to realize that wrongs could and would be set right within their institutions. We proved that democracy can work.

I have said to you that there is a very great difference between the two parties in what they do about Communism. Conditions congenial to Communism were being bred and fostered throughout this Nation up to the very day of March 4, 1933. Hunger was breeding it, loss of homes and farms was breeding it, closing banks were breeding it, a ruinous price level was breeding it. Discontent and fear were spreading through the land. The previous national Administration, bewildered, did nothing.

In their speeches, they deplored it, but by their actions, they encouraged it. The injustices, the inequalities, the downright suffering out of which revolutions come—what did they do about these things? Lacking courage, they evaded. Being selfish, they neglected. Being shortsighted, they ignored. When the crisis came—as these wrongs made it sure to come—America was unprepared.

Our lack of preparation for it was best proved by the cringing and the fear of the very people whose indifference helped to make the crisis. They came to us pleading that we should do, overnight, what they should have been doing through the years.

And the simple causes of our unpreparedness were two: First, a weak leadership, and, secondly, an inability to see causes, to understand the reasons for social unrest—the tragic plight of 90 percent of the men, women and children who made up the population of the United States.

* * *

Who is there in America who believes that we can run the risk of turning back our Government to the old leadership which brought it to the brink of 1933? Out of the strains and stresses of these years, we have come to see that the true conservative is the man who has a real concern for injustices and takes thought against the day of reckoning. The true conservative seeks to protect the system of private property and free enterprise by correcting such injustices and inequalities as arise from it. The most serious threat to our institutions comes from those who refuse to face the need for change. Liberalism becomes the protection for the far-sighted conservative.

Never has a Nation made greater strides in the safeguarding of democracy than we have made during the past three years. Wise and prudent men—intelligent conservatives—have long known that in a changing world worthy institutions can be conserved only by adjusting them to the changing time. In the words of the great essayist, "The voice of great events is proclaiming to us. Reform if you would preserve."

I am that kind of conservative because I am that kind of liberal.

CAMPAIGN SPEECH AT MADISON SQUARE GARDEN

October 31, 1936

Here is a catalog of objectives that comprise Roosevelt's philosophy of social justice. He lashed out at the misrepresentations and assaults on his administration's record from the right, which was looking for a return to the days of "indifferent" government. His impassioned defense, especially of social security legislation, responded to bitter attacks from unfriendly editorialists of a conservative press and groups like the Liberty League.

On the eve of the national election, it is well for us to stop for a moment and analyze calmly and without prejudice the effect on our nation of a victory by either of the major political parties. The problem of the electorate is far deeper, far more vital than the continuance in the presidency of any individual. For the greater issue goes beyond units of humanity—it goes to humanity itself.

In 1932, the issue was the restoration of American democracy; and the American people were in a mood to win. They did win. In 1936, the issue is the preservation of their victory. Again they are in a mood to win. Again they will win.

More than four years ago in accepting the Democratic nomination in Chicago, I said, "Give me your help not to win votes alone, but to win in this crusade to restore America to its own people."

The banners of that crusade still fly in the van of a nation that is on the march.

It is needless to repeat the details of the program which this Administration has been hammering out on the anvils of experience. No amount of misrepresentation or statistical contortion can conceal or blur or smear that record. Neither the attacks of unscrupulous enemies nor the exaggerations of over-zealous friends will serve to mislead the American people.

What was our hope in 1932? Above all other things the American people wanted peace. They wanted peace of mind instead of gnawing fear.

First, they sought escape from the personal terror which had stalked them for three years. They wanted the peace that comes from security in their homes: safety for their savings, permanence in their jobs, a fair profit from their enterprise.

Next, they wanted peace in the community, the peace that springs from the ability to meet the needs of community life: schools, playgrounds, parks, sanitation, highways—those things which are expected of solvent local government. They sought escape from disintegration and bankruptcy in local and state affairs.

They also sought peace within the nation: protection of their currency, fairer wages, the ending of long hours of toil, the abolition of child labor, the elimination of wild-cat speculation, the safety of their children from kidnappers.

* * *

We have not come this far without a struggle and I assure you we cannot go further without a struggle.

For 12 years this nation was afflicted with hear-nothing, see-nothing, do-nothing government. The nation looked to government but the government looked away. Nine mocking years with the golden calf and three long years of the scourge! Nine crazy years at the ticker and three long years in the breadlines! Nine mad years of mirage and three long years of despair! Powerful influences strive today to restore that kind of government with its doctrine that that government is best which is most indifferent.

For nearly four years, you have had an administration which instead of twirling its thumbs has rolled up its sleeves. We will keep our sleeves rolled up.

We had to struggle with the old enemies of peace—business and financial monopoly, speculation, reckless banking, class antagonism, sectionalism, war profiteering.

They had begun to consider the government of the United States as a mere appendage to their own affairs. We know now that government by organized money is just as dangerous as government by organized mob.

Never before in all our history have these forces been united against one candidate as they stand today. They are unanimous in their hate for me—and I welcome their hatred

I should like to have it said of my first Administration that in it the forces of selfishness and of lust for power met their match. I should like to have it said of my second administration that in it these forces met their master. . . .

Here is an amazing paradox! The very employers and politicians and publishers who talk most loudly of class antagonism and the destruction of the American system now undermine that system by this attempt to coerce the votes of the wage earners of this country. It is the 1936 version of the old threat to close down the factory or the office if a particular candidate does not win. It is an old strategy of tyrants to delude their victims into fighting their battles for them.

Every message in a pay envelope, even if it is the truth, is a command to vote according to the will of the employer. But this propaganda is worse—it is deceit.

They tell the worker his wage will be reduced by a contribution to some vague form of old-age insurance. They carefully conceal from him the fact that for every dollar of premium he pays for that insurance, the employer pays another dollar. That omission is deceit.

They carefully conceal from him the fact that under the federal law, he receives another insurance policy to help him if he loses his job, and that the premium of that policy is paid 100 percent by the employer and not one cent by the worker. They do not tell him that the insurance policy that is bought for him is far more favorable to him than any policy that any private insurance company could afford to issue. That omission is deceit.

They imply to him that he pays all the cost of both forms of insurance. They carefully conceal from him the fact that for every dollar put up by him his employer puts up three dollars—three for one. And that omission is deceit.

But they are guilty of more than deceit. When they imply that the reserves thus created against both these policies will be stolen by some future Congress, diverted to some wholly foreign purpose, they attack the integrity and honor of American government itself. Those who suggest that are already aliens to the spirit of American democracy. Let them emigrate and try their lot under some foreign flag in which they have more confidence.

The fraudulent nature of this attempt is well shown by the record of votes on the passage of the Social Security Act. In addition to an overwhelming majority of Democrats in both Houses, 77 Republican Representatives voted for it and only 18 against it and 15 Republican Senators voted for it and only five against it. Where does this last-minute drive of the Republican leadership leave these Republican Representatives and Senators who helped enact this law?

I am sure the vast majority of law-abiding businessmen who are not parties to this propaganda fully appreciate extent of the threat to honest business contained in this coercion.

I have expressed indignation at this form of campaigning and I am confident that the overwhelming majority of employers, workers and the general public share that indignation and will show it at the polls on Tuesday next. . . .

It is because I have sought to think in terms of the whole nation that I am confident that today, just as four years ago, the people want more than promises.

Our vision for the future contains more than promises.

This is our answer to those who, silent about their own plans, ask us to state our objectives.

Of course we will continue to seek to improve working conditions for the workers of America—to reduce hours over-long, to increase wages that spell starvation, to end the labor of children, to wipe out sweatshops. Of course, we will continue every effort to end monopoly in business, to support collective bargaining, to stop unfair competition, to abolish dishonorable trade practices. For all these we have only just begun to fight.

Of course, we will continue to work for cheaper electricity in the homes and on the farms of America, for better and cheaper transportation, for low interest rates, for sounder home financing, for better banking, for the regulation of security issues, for reciprocal trade among nations, for the wiping out of slums. For all these we have only just begun to fight.

Of course, we will continue our efforts in behalf of the farmers of America. With their continued cooperation, we will do all in our power to end the piling up of huge surpluses which spelled ruinous prices for their crops. We will persist in successful action for better land use, for reforestation, for the conservation of water all the way from its source to the sea, for drought and flood control, for better marketing facilities for farm commodities, for a definite reduction of farm tenancy, for encouragement of farmer cooperatives, for crop insurance and a stable food supply. For all these we have only just begun to fight.

Of course, we will provide useful work for the needy unemployed; we prefer useful work to the pauperism of a dole.

Here and now, I want to make myself clear about those who disparage their fellow citizens on the relief rolls. They say that those on relief are not merely jobless—that they are worthless. Their solution for the relief problem is to end relief—to purge the rolls by starvation. To use the language of the stock broker our needy unemployed would be cared for when, as, and if some fairy godmother should happen on the scene.

You and I will continue to refuse to accept that estimate of our unemployed fellow Americans. Your government is still on the same side of the street with the Good Samaritan and not with those who pass by on the other side.

Again—what of our objectives?

Of course, we will continue our efforts for young men and women so that they may obtain an education and an opportunity to put it to use. Of course we will continue our help for the crippled, for the blind, for the mothers, our insurance for the unemployed, our security for the aged. Of course, we will continue to protect the consumer against unnecessary price spreads, against the costs that are added by monopoly and speculation. We will continue our successful efforts to increase his purchasing power and to keep it constant.

For these things, too, and for a multitude of others like them, we have only just begun to fight.

All this—all these objectives—spell peace at home. All our actions, all our ideals, spell also peace with other nations.

Today there is war and rumor of war. We want none of it. But while we guard our shores against threats of war, we will continue to remove the causes of unrest and antagonism at home which might make our people easier victims to those for whom foreign war is profitable. You know well that those who stand to profit by war are not on our side in this campaign.

"Peace on earth, good will toward men"—democracy must cling to that message. For it is my deep conviction that democracy cannot live without that true religion which gives a nation a sense of justice and of moral purpose. Above our political forums, above our market places stand the altars of our faith—altars on which burn the fires of devotion that maintain all that is best in us and all that is best in our nation.

We have need of that devotion today. It is that which makes it possible for government to persuade those who are mentally prepared to fight each other to go on instead to work for and to sacrifice for each other. That is why we need to say with the prophet, "What doth the Lord require of thee—but to do justly, to love mercy, and to walk humbly with thy God." That is why the recovery we seek, the recovery we are winning, is more than economic. In it are included justice and love and humility, not for ourselves as individuals alone, but for our nation. That is the road to peace.

SECOND INAUGURAL ADDRESS

January 20, 1937

*On this as in other important occasions Roosevelt tied the work of his admin-
istration to that of the founding fathers, connecting the constitutional refer-
ence to the "general welfare" with the obligation of modern government to
work for the basic economic security of its people. He defended the power of
government to do this work as fully compatible with democracy and repeated
his objection to the influence of private power over the public welfare. This
was a response to critics who identified Roosevelt and the New Deal with the
erosion of democracy.*

* * *

This year marks the 150th anniversary of the Constitutional Convention which made us a nation. At that Convention, our forefathers
found the way out of the chaos which followed the Revolutionary War;
they created a strong government with powers of united action sufficient then and now to solve problems utterly beyond individual or
local solution. A century and a half ago they established the federal
government in order to promote the general welfare and secure the
blessings of liberty to the American people. Today we invoke those
same powers of government to achieve the same objectives.

Four years of new experience have not belied our historic instinct.
They hold out the clear hope that government within communities,
government within the separate states, and government of the United
States can do the things the times require, without yielding its democracy. Our tasks in the last four years did not force democracy to take a
holiday.

Nearly all of us recognize that as intricacies of human relationships
increase, so power to govern them also must increase—power to stop
evil; power to do good. The essential democracy of our nation and
the safety of our people depend not upon the absence of power, but
upon lodging it with those whom the people can change or continue
at stated intervals through an honest and free system of elections. The
Constitution of 1787 did not make our democracy impotent.

In fact, in these last four years, we have made the exercise of all
power more democratic; for we have begun to bring private autocratic
powers into their proper subordination to the public's government.

The legend that they were invincible—above and beyond the processes of a democracy—has been shattered. They have been challenged and beaten.

Our progress out of the depression is obvious. But that is not all that you and I mean by the new order of things. Our pledge was not merely to do a patchwork job with second-hand materials. By using the new materials of social justice, we have undertaken to erect on the old foundations a more enduring structure for the better use of future generations.

* * *

I see a great nation, upon a great continent, blessed with a great wealth of natural resources. Its hundred and thirty million people are at peace among themselves; they are making their country a good neighbor among the nations. I see a United States which can demonstrate that, under democratic methods of government, national wealth can be translated into a spreading volume of human comforts hitherto unknown, and the lowest standard of living can be raised far above the level of mere subsistence.

But here is the challenge to our democracy: In this nation I see tens of millions of its citizens—a substantial part of its whole population—who at this very moment are denied the greater part of what the very lowest standards of today call the necessities of life.

I see millions of families trying to live on incomes so meager that the pall of family disaster hangs over them day by day.

I see millions whose daily lives in city and on farm continue under conditions labeled indecent by a so-called polite society half a century ago.

I see millions denied education, recreation, and the opportunity to better their lot and the lot of their children.

I see millions lacking the means to buy the products of farm and factory and by their poverty denying work and productiveness to many other millions.

I see one-third of a nation ill-housed, ill-clad, ill-nourished.

It is not in despair that I paint you that picture. I paint it for you in hope—because the nation, seeing and understanding the injustice in it, proposes to paint it out. We are determined to make every American citizen the subject of his country's interest and concern; and we will never regard any faithful, law-abiding group within our borders as superfluous. The test of our progress is not whether we add more to the abundance of those who have much; it is whether we provide enough for those who have too little.

If I know aught of the spirit and purpose of our nation, we will not listen to Comfort, Opportunism, and Timidity. We will carry on.

Overwhelmingly, we of the Republic are men and women of good will; men and women who have more than warm hearts of dedication; men and women who have cool heads and willing hands of practical purpose as well. They will insist that every agency of popular government use effective instruments to carry out their will.

Government is competent when all who compose it work as trustees for the whole people. It can make constant progress when it keeps abreast of all the facts. It can obtain justified support and legitimate criticism when the people receive true information of all that government does.

If I know aught of the will of our people, they will demand that these conditions of effective government shall be created and maintained. They will demand a nation uncorrupted by cancers of injustice and, therefore, strong among the nations in its example of the will to peace.

Today we re-consecrate our country to long-cherished ideals in a suddenly changed civilization. In every land there are always at work forces that drive men apart and forces that draw men together. In our personal ambitions we are individualists. But in our seeking for economic and political progress as a nation, we all go up, or else we all go down, as one people.

* * *

WAGES AND HOURS

Message to Congress, May 24, 1937

During the decade of the 1920s, the United States had organized everything necessary for a thriving consumer economy—except a sufficiently large body of consumers. This contributed much to the eventual economic collapse. At the start of his second term, Roosevelt sought to expand the purchasing power of the working class. An ironic political hurdle in this effort came from the resistance of some leaders of organized labor to minimum wage legislation on the grounds that a legislated minimum would be regarded as a standard or maximum wage. In March, the Supreme Court had reversed its position of a year earlier on the constitutionality of a state minimum wage law. The timing was right for launching the administration's plan for wages and hours legislation. In this message to Congress, Roosevelt was more generous to his conservative opposition in ascribing "good intentions" to them than they were in frequently excoriating his intentions as un-American.

The time has arrived for us to take further action to extend the frontiers of social progress. Such further action initiated by the legislative branch of the government, administered by the executive, and sustained by the judicial, is within the common sense framework and purpose of our Constitution and receives beyond doubt the approval of our electorate.

The overwhelming majority of our population earns its daily bread either in agriculture or in industry. One-third of our population, the overwhelming majority of which is in agriculture or industry, is ill-nourished, ill-clad and ill-housed.

The overwhelming majority of this nation has little patience with that small minority which vociferates today that prosperity has returned, that wages are good, that crop prices are high and that government should take a holiday.

The truth of the matter, of course, is that the exponents of the theory of private initiative as the cure for deep-seated national ills want in most cases to improve the lot of mankind. But, well intentioned as they may be, they fail for four evident reasons—first, they see the problem from the point of view of their own business; second, they see the problem from the point of view of their own locality or region; third, they cannot act unanimously because they have no machinery for agreeing among themselves; and, finally, they have no power to bind the inevitable minority of chiselers within their own ranks.

Though we may go far in admitting the innate decency of this small minority, the whole story of our nation proves that social progress has too often been fought by them. In actual practice, it has been effectively advanced only by the passage of laws by state legislatures or the national Congress.

Today, you and I are pledged to take further steps to reduce the lag in the purchasing power of industrial workers and to strengthen and stabilize the markets for the farmers' products. The two go hand in hand. Each depends for its effectiveness upon the other. Both working simultaneously will open new outlets for productive capital. Our nation so richly endowed with natural resources and with a capable and industrious population should be able to devise ways and means of insuring to all our able-bodied working men and women a fair day's pay for a fair day's work. A self-supporting and self-respecting democracy can plead no justification for the existence of child labor, no economic reason for chiseling workers' wages or stretching workers' hours.

Enlightened business is learning that competition ought not to cause bad social consequences which inevitably react upon the profits of business itself. All but the hopelessly reactionary will agree that to conserve our primary resources of manpower, government must have some control over maximum hours, minimum wages, the evil of child labor and the exploitation of unorganized labor.

* * *

We know that over-work and under-pay do not increase the national income when a large portion of our workers remain unemployed. Reasonable and flexible use of the long-established right of government to set and to change working hours can, I hope, decrease unemployment in those groups in which unemployment today principally exists.

Our problem is to work out in practice those labor standards which will permit the maximum but prudent employment of our human resources to bring within the reach of the average man and woman a maximum of goods and of services conducive to the fulfillment of the promise of American life.

Legislation can, I hope, be passed at this session of the Congress further to help those who toil in factory and on farm. We have promised it. We cannot stand still.

CAMPAIGN ADDRESS AT BROOKLYN

November 1, 1940

The president enjoyed the scramble of partisan politics at election time, especially when he could catch one of the opposition in an insensitive gaff. Here he blasted Republicans as defenders of privilege. Campaigning for an unprecedented third term, he reaffirmed his commitment to private enterprise as well as his agenda of equal opportunity and social justice.

* * *

We all remember how negligible was the opposition that this Administration met in the early days [of the New Deal] when it was cleaning up the wreckage which had come from the era of speculation.

The bitter opposition from Republican leaders did not come until a little later. It came when this Administration made it clear that we were not merely salvaging a few things from the past, but that we were determined to make our system of private enterprise and private profit work more efficiently, more democratically, to fill the demands and needs of all the people of this land.

We understand the philosophy of those who offer resistance, of those who conduct a counteroffensive against the American people's march of social progress. It is not an opposition which comes necessarily from wickedness—it is an opposition that comes from subconscious resistance to any measure that disturbs the position of privilege.

It is an unfortunate human failing that a full pocketbook often groans more loudly than an empty stomach.

I am, as you know, a firm believer in private enterprise and in private property. I am a firm believer in the American opportunity of men and women to rise in private enterprise.

But, of course, if private opportunity is to remain safe, average men and women must be able to have it as a part of their own individual satisfaction in life and their own stake in democracy.

With that in view, we have pushed ahead with social and economic reforms, determined that this period in American life should be written down as an heroic era—an era in which men fought not merely to preserve a past, but to build a future.

You and I have seen nations, great and small, go down in ruin, or get backed up against the wall, because the reactionary men who led them could not see the real danger that threatened. They were afraid of losing their own selfish privilege and power.

* * *

Our program in the past, our program for the future, is, as you know, equality of economic opportunity. Such a program calls for many things. It requires an orderly settlement of industrial disputes not by those devoted to company unions, but by agencies alert to the requirements of labor and mindful of the responsibilities of industry.

This program entails old-age insurance and unemployment insurance, operating on an increasingly wider base, so that eventually it will include every man and woman in the country.

It makes available cheap credit to impoverished tenants, to consumers, and to small business. In fact, it has always seemed to me that our program starts with small business, so that it may grow and flourish.

It curbs the old predatory activities of high finance and monopoly practices.

It guarantees that our national resources are used for the benefit of the whole people—and not exploited for the benefit of a few.

It provides for the resettlement of farmers from marginal lands to richer lands, and for farm ownership for enslaved tenants.

Monopoly does not like this program. Certain types of high finance do not like it. Most of the American plutocracy do not like it.

But the vast majority of American business, the backbone of American business, continues to grow and flourish under it. For that, business is interested in reasonable profits, not in promoters' tribute. That business is interested in freedom from monopolistic restraints and economic imperialism. That business knows that the farmers and the workers, the great mass of our citizens, have never asked for more than equality and fair play.

* * *

The true attitude of some leaders of the Republican Party toward the common man is not frequently revealed, but occasionally their true feelings break through the restraints which a political campaign places upon their tongues, and suddenly they misspeak themselves. We can then see their true sentiments in all their naked unloveliness.

In a Republican campaign speech the other day, a prominent leader of the Philadelphia bar delivered himself in these words, quoted in *The New York Times.*

"The President's only supporters," he said, "are paupers, those who earn less than $1,200 a year and aren't worth *that,* and the Roosevelt family."

I think we might just as well forget the Roosevelt family, but these Americans whom this man calls "paupers," these Americans who, in his view, are not worth the income they receive, small though it is—who are they? They are only millions and millions of American families, constituting a very large part of the nation! They are only the common men and women who have helped build this country, whose labors made it great, and who would defend it with their lives when need arose.

The demand for social and economic justice comes from those who receive less than $1,200 a year, but not from them alone. For I believe that when Americans cross this dividing line of $100 a month, they do not lose their devotion to social and economic justice.

They do not suddenly become greedy and selfish. And I count among my supporters millions of other men and women who vote by the dictates of their hearts and minds, and not by the size of their bank accounts.

"Paupers" who are not worth their salt—there speaks the true sentiment of the Republican leadership in this year of grace.

Can the Republican leaders deny that all this all-too-prevailing Republican sentiment is a direct, vicious, unpatriotic appeal to class hatred and class contempt?

That, my friends, is just what I am fighting against with all my heart and soul.

I am only fighting for a free America—for a country in which all men and women have equal rights to liberty and justice.

I am fighting against the revival of government by special privilege—government by lobbyists—government vested in the hands of those who favor and who would have us imitate the foreign dictatorships.

I am fighting, as I always have fought, for the rights of the little man as well as the big man—for the weak as well as the strong, for those who are helpless as well as for those who can help themselves.

I am fighting to keep this nation prosperous and at peace. I am fighting to keep our people out of foreign wars, and to keep foreign conceptions of government out of our own United States.

I am fighting for these great and good causes. I am fighting to defend them against the power and might of those who now rise up to challenge them. And I will not stop fighting.

STATE OF THE UNION MESSAGE

January 11, 1944

The war, heading for its climax, occupied much of the president's time and his State of the Union address. But even with the heavy concerns of a victory strategy and post-war planning, Roosevelt never lost sight of economic ideals to which he had been so long committed. Despite a new prosperity born of wartime full-employment, too many Americans remained insecure. People in need are not fully free, and as the Bill of Rights protected civil liberties, he proposed here an economic bill of rights *to assure social justice free of discrimination.*

* * *

It is our duty now to begin to lay the plans and determine the strategy for the winning of a lasting peace and the establishment of an American standard of living higher than ever before known. We cannot be content, no matter how high that general standard of living may be, if some fraction of our people—whether it be one-third or one-fifth or one-tenth—is ill-fed, ill-clothed, ill-housed, and insecure.

This Republic had its beginning, and grew to its present strength, under the protection of certain inalienable political rights—among them the right of free speech, free press, free worship, trial by jury, freedom from unreasonable searches and seizures. They were our rights to life and liberty. As our nation has grown in size and stature, however—as our industrial economy expanded—these political rights proved inadequate to assure us equality in the pursuit of happiness.

We have come to a clear realization of the fact that true individual freedom cannot exist without economic security and independence. "Necessitous men are not free men." People who are hungry and out of a job are the stuff of which dictatorships are made.

In our day these economic truths have become accepted as self-evident. We have accepted, so to speak, a second Bill of Rights under which a new basis of security and prosperity can be established for all—regardless of station, race, or creed. Among these are:

The right to a useful and remunerative job in the industries or shops or farms or mines of the Nation;

The right to earn enough to provide adequate food and clothing and recreation;

The right of every farmer to raise and sell his products at a return which will give him and his family a decent living;

The right of every businessman, large and small, to trade in an atmosphere of freedom from unfair competition and domination by monopolies at home or abroad;

The right of every family to a decent home;

The right to adequate medical care and the opportunity to achieve and enjoy good health;

The right to adequate protection from the economic fears of old age, sickness, accident, and unemployment;

The right to a good education.

All of these rights spell security. And after this war is won we must be prepared to move forward, in the implementation of these rights, to new goals of human happiness and well-being.

* * *

CAMPAIGN ADDRESS

Soldier Field, Chicago, October 28, 1944

During his campaign for reelection, Roosevelt reminded voters of his hopes for an Economic Bill of Rights as an agenda for the future. Victory in the war was in sight and planning for the post-war world was much on the president's mind, but he was also thinking of the course of American life at home when the fighting stopped. Clearly, his objective was to continue and complete the work of the New Deal.

* * *

Tonight I want to talk simply to you about the future of America. . . .

For the American people are resolved that when our men and women return home from this war, they shall come back to the best possible place on the face of the earth—they shall come back to a place where all persons, regardless of race, color, creed or place of birth, can live in peace and honor and human dignity—free to speak, free to pray as they wish—free from want—and free from fear.

Last January, in my message to the Congress on the State of the Union, I outlined an Economic Bill of Rights on which "a new basis of security and prosperity can be established for all."

* * *

Now, what do those rights mean? They "spell security. And after this war is won we must be prepared to move forward, in the implementation of these rights, to new goals of human happiness and well-being."

Some people—I need not name them—have sneered at these ideals as well as at the ideals of the Atlantic Charter, the ideals of the Four Freedoms. They have said that they were the dreams of starry-eyed New Dealers—that it is silly to talk of them because we cannot attain these ideals tomorrow or the next day.

The American people have greater faith than that. I know that they agree with these objectives—that they demand them—that they are determined to get them—and that they are *going* to get them. The American people have a good habit—the habit of going right ahead and accomplishing the impossible.

* * *

When we think of the America of tomorrow, we think of many things.

One of them is the American home—in our cities, in our villages, on our farms. Millions of our people have never had homes worthy of American standards—well-built homes, with electricity and plumbing, air and sunlight.

The demand for homes and our capacity to build them call for a program of well over a million homes a year for at least ten years. Private industry can build and finance the vast majority of these homes. Government can and will assist and encourage private industry to do this, as it has for many years. For those very low income groups that cannot possibly afford decent homes, the Federal Government should continue to assist local housing authorities in meeting that need.

In the future America that we are talking about, we think of new highways, new parkways. We think of thousands of new airports to service the new commercial and private air travel which is bound to come after the war. We think of new planes, large and small, new cheap automobiles with low maintenance and operation costs. We think of new hospitals and new health clinics. We think of a new merchant marine for our expanded world trade.

My friends, think of these vast possibilities for industrial expansion—and you will foresee opportunities for more millions of jobs.

And with all that, our Economic Bill of Rights—like the sacred Bill of Rights of our Constitution itself—must be applied to all our citizens, irrespective of race, or creed, or color.

* * *

Notes

Chapter 1: The First Revolution

1. Frederick Jackson Turner, "The Significance of the Frontier in American History," American Historical Association, Annual Report, 1893.

2. Gordon S. Wood, *The Radicalism of the American Revolution* (New York: Alfred A. Knopf, 1992), 113.

3. Mario R. DiNunzio, *American Democracy and the Authoritarian Tradition of the West* (Lanham, MD: University Press of America, 1987), 98.

4. Gordon S. Wood, *The Creation of the American Republic 1776–1787* (Chapel Hill: University of North Carolina Press, 1969), 601.

Chapter 2: The Second Revolution

1. Eric Foner, *Reconstruction* (New York: Harper and Row Publishers, 1988), 192.

2. James M. McPherson, *Abraham Lincoln and the Second American Revolution* (New York: Oxford University Press, 1991), 138.

3. Foner, 278–279.

Chapter 3: Roots

1. Richard Hofstadter, *The Age of Reform*, (New York: Alfred A. Knopf, 1955), 286ff.

2. Arthur M. Schlesinger, Jr., *The Crisis of the Old Order* (Boston: Houghton Mifflin Company, 1957), 141, 436.

Chapter 4: The Mind of FDR

1. Frank Freidel, *Franklin D. Roosevelt: A Rendezvous with Destiny* (Boston: Little Brown and Co., 1990), 16–17; Frank Friedel, *Launching the New Deal* (Boston: Little Brown and Co., 1973), 64; Arthur M. Schlesinger, Jr., *The Politics of Upheaval* (Boston: Houghton Mifflin Company, 1960), 647.

2. William E. Leuchtenburg, *The FDR Years* (New York: Columbia University Press, 1995), 3; Schlesinger, *Upheaval*, 647; Anthony F. Badger, *FDR: The First Hundred Days* (New York: Hill and Wang, 2008), 6.

3. Wilmon H. Droze, George Wolfskill, William E. Leuchtenburg, *Essays on the New Deal* (Austin: University of Texas Press, 1969), 53; Robert S. McElvaine, *Franklin Delano Roosevelt* (Washington, DC: Congressional Quarterly Press, 2002), 307.

4. Frances Perkins, *The Roosevelt I Knew* (New York: The Viking Press, 1946), 330.

5. Franklin D. Roosevelt, *The Public Papers and Addresses of Franklin D. Roosevelt*, S. I. Rosenman, comp. (New York: Random House, Macmillan, Harper & Bros. 1938–1950), Vol. 1, 646.

6. Rexford G. Tugwell, *FDR: Architect of an Era* (New York: The Macmillan Co., 1967), 113–114.

7. Frank Friedel, *Franklin D. Roosevelt The Apprenticeship* (Boston: Little Brown and Company, 1952), 94.

8. Ibid., 37.

9. Elliott Roosevelt, ed., *The Roosevelt Letters*, Vol. 1 (London: George G. Harrap & Co., 1949), 46.

10. Rexford G. Tugwell, *The Democratic Roosevelt* (Garden City, NY: Doubleday and Co., 1957), 233.

11. Thomas H. Greer, *What Roosevelt Thought* (East Lansing, MI: Michigan State University Press, 1958), 4–9; Perkins, 141, 144.

12. Joseph P. Lash, *Eleanor and Franklin* (New York: W. W. Norton & Co., 1971), 391; Eleanor Roosevelt, *This I Remember* (New York: Harper and Brothers, 1949), 69, 346; Perkins, 143–144.

13. Quoted in Arthur M. Schlesinger, Jr., *The Crisis of the Old Order* (Boston: Houghton Mifflin Company, 1957), 480.

14. Freidel, *Rendezvous*, 15.

15. Alan Lawson, *A Commonwealth of Hope: The New Deal Response to Crisis* (Baltimore: Johns Hopkins University Press, 2006), 37–38.

16. Perkins, 29–30.

17. *Public Papers*, Vol. 1, 35–36, 59.

18. *Public Papers*, Vol. 1, 456–457; Freidel, *Rendezvous*, 61.

19. "The Social Age," Phi Beta Kappa Address, June 17, 1929, Franklin D. Roosevelt Library.

20. Conrad Black, *Franklin Delano Roosevelt: Champion of Freedom* (New York: Public Affairs, 2003), 216–217.

21. Schlesinger, *Crisis*, 393.

22. Schlesinger, *Upheaval*, 651.

23. Tugwell, *FDR*, 96.

24. *Public Papers*, Vol. 1, 861, 458–459, 778.

25. Mario Einaudi, *The Roosevelt Revolution* (Westport, CT: Greenwood Press, 1959), 68, 73; Perkins, 166.

26. *Public Papers*, Vol. 1, 758.

27. *Public Papers*, Vol. 3, 288, 292.

28. *Public Papers*, Vol. 3, 483.

29. *Public Papers*, Vol. 4, 17.

30. *Public Papers*, 1937, 1–5.

31. *Public Papers*, 1940, 534.

32. *Public Papers*, 1944–45, 371.

33. Richard Hofstadter, *The American Political Tradition and the Men Who Made It* (New York: Vintage Books, 1958), 335.

Chapter 5: The Third Revolution—Phase I

1. W. H. Brands, *Traitor to His Class* (New York: Doubleday, 2008), 242f.

2. Franklin D. Roosevelt, *Public Papers and Addresses of Franklin D. Roosevelt*, Samuel I. Rosenman, comp. (New York: Random House, Macmillan, Harper and Bros., 1938–1950), Vol. 1, 625.

3. James MacGregor Burns, *Roosevelt: The Lion and the Fox* (New York: Harcourt, Brace & World, 1956), 151; Schlesinger, *Crisis*, 291.

4. *Public Papers*, Vol. 1, 646.

5. Rexford G. Tugwell, *In Search of Roosevelt* (Cambridge: Harvard University Press, 1972), 175–176.

6. *Public Papers*, Vol. 1, 742–756, 778–779, 786–794.

7. *Public Papers*, Vol. 1, 649.

8. James T. Patterson, *Congressional Conservatism and the New Deal* (Lexington, KY: University of Kentucky Press, 1967), 4–6.

9. Arthur M. Schlesinger, Jr., *The Coming of the New Deal* (Boston: Houghton Mifflin Company, 1959), 5.

10. Badger, Anthony F. Badger, *FDR: The First Hundred Days* (New York: Hill and Wang, 2008), 80.

11. Mario Einaudi, *The Roosevelt Revolution* (Westport, CT: Greenwood Press, 1959), 83.

12. Arthur M. Schlesinger, Jr., *The Crisis of the Old Order 1919–1933* (Boston: Houghton Mifflin, 1957), 249; David M. Kennedy, *Freedom from Fear: The*

American People in Depression and War (New York: Oxford University Press, 1999), 163.

13. Arthur M. Schlesinger, Jr., *The Politics of Upheaval* (Boston: Houghton Mifflin, 1960), 268.

14. Schlesinger, *Coming of the New Deal*, 338; John A. Salmond, *The Civilian Conservation Corps, 1933–1942* (Durham, NC: Duke University Press, 1967), 220–221; Frank Freidel, *Launching the New Deal* (Boston: Little Brown and Company, 1973), 266.

15. Elliott Roosevelt and James Brough, *The Roosevelts of the White House: A Rendezvous With Destiny* (New York: G. P. Putnam's Sons, 1975), 70.

Chapter 6: The Third Revolution—Phase II

1. Arthur M. Schlesinger, Jr., *The Politics of Upheaval* (Boston: Houghton Mifflin, 1960), 443.

2. William E. Leuchtenburg, *Franklin D. Roosevelt and the New Deal 1932–1940* (New York: Harper and Row, 1963), 124–126; Schlesinger, *Upheaval*, 345–347; Jean Edward Smith, *FDR* (New York: Random House, 2007), 355–356.

3. Schlesinger, *Upheaval*, 356–357.

4. Smith, 320–321.

5. Leuchtenburg, *New Deal*, 151; Frances Perkins, *The Roosevelt I Knew* (New York: The Viking Press, 1946), 239, 308.

6. Franklin D. Roosevelt, *Public Papers and Addresses of Franklin D. Roosevelt*, Samuel I. Rosenman, comp. (New York: Random House, Macmillan, Harper and Bros., 1938–1950), Vol. 4, 270ff.

7. Perkins, 301.

8. Sylvester J. Schieber and John B. Shoven, *The Real Deal: The History and Future of Social Security* (New Haven: Yale University Press, 1999), 37.

9. Quoted in Arthur M. Schlesinger, Jr., *The Coming of the New Deal* (Boston: Houghton Mifflin, 1959), 308–309.

10. *Public Papers,* Vol. 4, 18.

11. Quoted in Schlesinger, *Coming of the New Deal*, 311.

12. Schieber and Shoven, 53.

13. Schlesinger, *Coming of the New Deal*, 308–311; Schieber and Shoren, 79.

14. *Public Papers,* Vol. 5, 233–234, 390, 568.

15. James McGregor Burns, *Roosevelt: The Lion and the Fox* (New York: Harcourt, Brace & World, 1956), 266–267.

16. *Public Papers,* 1937, 210–211.

17. Perkins, 257–258; *Public Papers,* 1937, 496.

18. Perkins, 260.

19. *Public Papers,* 1938, 6.

20. James T. Patterson, *Congressional Conservatism and the New Deal* (Lexington: University of Kentucky Press, 1967), 23, 325–326.

21. Conrad Black, *Franklin Delano Roosevelt: Champion of Freedom* (New York: Public Affairs, 2003), 436; Frank Freidel, *Franklin D. Roosevelt: A Rendezvous with Destiny* (Boston: Little Brown and Company, 1990), 256.

22. *Public Papers*, 1943, 450–451.

23. Alan Lawson, *A Commonwealth of Hope: The New Deal Response to Crisis* (Baltimore: Johns Hopkins University Press, 2006), 240.

Chapter 7: Counterrevolutionaries

1. William E. Leuchtenburg, *The FDR Years* (New York: Columbia University Press, 1995), 2.

2. Quoted in Arthur M. Schlesinger, Jr., *The Politics of Upheaval* (Boston: Houghton Mifflin, 1960), 180.

3. T. Harry Williams, *Huey Long* (New York: Alfred A. Knopf, 1969), 844.

4. Glen Jeansonne, *Gerald L. K. Smith, Minister of Hate* (New Haven: Yale University Press, 1988), 47, 59.

5. David H. Bennett, *Demagogues in the Depression* (New Brunswick, NJ: Rutgers University Press, 1969), 224–225; Charles Tull, *Father Coughlin and the New Deal* (Syracuse: Syracuse University Press, 1965), 73; Donald Warren, *Radio Priest* (New York: Free Press, 1996), 92.

6. Schlesinger, *Upheaval*, 633.

7. W. H. Brands, *Traitor to His Class* (New York: Doubleday, 2008), 451; Richard O'Connor, *The First Hurrah: A Biography of Alfred E. Smith* (New York: G. P. Putman, 1970), 282–285.

Chapter 8: The Legacy and the Challenge

1. William E. Leuchtenburg, *The FDR Years* (New York: Columbia University Press, 1995), 279–280.

2. James McGregor Burns, *Roosevelt: The Lion and the Fox* (New York: Harcourt, Brace & World, 1956), 208.

3. Elliott Roosevelt and James Brough, *The Roosevelts of the White House: Rendezvous with Destiny* (New York: G. P. Putnam's Sons, 1975), 141.

4. Ronald Edsford, *The New Deal America's Response to the Great Depression* (Oxford: Blackwell Publishers, 2000), 286; Eric Goldman, *Rendezvous with Destiny* (New York: Vintage Books, 1956), 288; Patrick Renshaw, *Franklin D. Roosevelt* (New York: Longman, 2004), 191.

5. Franklin D. Roosevelt, *Public Papers and Addresses of Franklin D. Roosevelt*, Samuel I. Rosenman, comp. (New York: Random House, Macmillan, Harper and Bros., 1938–1950), 1944, 41.

6. John Kenneth Galbraith, *The Affluent Society* (Boston: Houghton Mifflin Co., 1958), 257.

Bibliography

Alter, Jonathan, *The Defining Moment: FDR's Hundred Days and the Triumph of Hope*. New York: Simon and Schuster, 2006.

Badger, Anthony F., *FDR: The First Hundred Days*. New York: Hill and Wang, 2008.

Bennett, David H., *Demagogues in the Depression*. New Brunswick, NJ: Rutgers University Press, 1969.

Black, Conrad, *Franklin Delano Roosevelt: Champion of Freedom*. New York: Public Affairs, 2003.

Brands, W. H., *Traitor to His Class*. New York: Doubleday, 2008.

Brinkley, Alan, *Voices of Protest: Huey Long, Father Coughlin, and the Great Depression*. New York: Vintage Books, 1982.

Burns, James McGregor, *Roosevelt: the Lion and the Fox*. New York: Harcourt, Brace & World, 1956.

Conkin, Paul K., *FDR and the Origins of the Welfare State*. New York: Thomas Y. Crowell Co., 1967.

Conkin, Paul K., *The New Deal*. New York: Thomas Y. Crowell Co., 1967.

DiNunzio, Mario R., *American Democracy and the Authoritarian Tradition of the West*. Lanham, MD: University Press of America, 1987.

Droze, Wilmon H., George Wolfskill, and William E. Leuchtenburg, *Essays on the New Deal*. Austin, TX: University of Texas Press, 1969.

Edsford, Ronald, *The New Deal: America's Response to the Great Depression*. Oxford, UK: Blackwell Publishers, 2000.

Einaudi, Mario, *The Roosevelt Revolution*. Westport, CT: Greenwood Press, 1959.

Flynn, George Q., *American Catholics & the Roosevelt Presidency 1932–1936*. Lexington, KY: University of Kentucky Press, 1968.

Freidel, Frank, *Franklin D. Roosevelt: A Rendezvous with Destiny*. Boston: Little Brown and Company, 1990.

Freidel, Frank, *Franklin D. Roosevelt: The Apprenticeship.* Boston: Little Brown and Company, 1952.

Freidel, Frank, *Launching the New Deal.* Boston: Little Brown and Company, 1973.

Frisch, Morton J., *Franklin D. Roosevelt.* Boston: Twayne Publishers, 1975.

Galbraith, John Kenneth, *The Affluent Society.* Boston: Houghton Mifflin, 1958.

Galbraith, John Kenneth, *The Great Crash.* Boston: Houghton Mifflin, 1955.

Goldman, Eric, *Rendezvous with Destiny.* New York: Vintage Books, 1956.

Greer, Thomas H., *What Roosevelt Thought.* East Lansing: Michigan State University Press, 1958.

Hofstadter, Richard, *The American Political Tradition and the Men Who Made It.* New York: Vintage Books, 1954.

Jeansonne, Glen, *Gerald L. K. Smith: Minister of Hate.* New Haven: Yale University Press, 1988.

Kennedy, David M., *Freedom from Fear: The American People in Depression and War 1929–1945.* New York: Oxford University Press, 1999.

Lawson, Alan, *A Commonwealth of Hope: The New Deal Response to Crisis.* Baltimore: Johns Hopkins University Press, 2006.

Leuchtenburg, William E., *Franklin D. Roosevelt and the New Deal 1932–1940.* New York: Harper and Row, 1963.

Leuchtenburg, William E., *The FDR Years.* New York: Columbia University Press, 1995.

Levine, Lawrence W., and Cornelia R. Levine, *The People and the President.* Boston: Beacon Press, 2002.

Link, William A., and Arthur S. Link, *American Epoch*, Vol. I. New York: McGraw Hill, 1993.

McElvaine, Robert S., *Franklin Delano Roosevelt.* Washington, DC: Congressional Quarterly Press, 2002.

McElvaine, Robert S., *The Great Depression: America 1929–1941.* New York: Times Books, 1984.

McKinley, Charles M., and Robert W. Frase, *Launching Social Security 1935–1937.* Madison: University of Wisconsin Press, 1970.

McPherson, James M., *Abraham Lincoln and the Second American Revolution.* New York: Oxford University Press, 1991.

O'Connor, Richard, *The First Hurrah: A Biography of Alfred E. Smith.* New York: G. P. Putnam & Sons, 1970.

Patterson, James T., *Congressional Conservatism and the New Deal.* Lexington: University of Kentucky Press, 1967.

Perkins, Frances, *The Roosevelt I Knew.* New York: The Viking Press, 1946.

Renshaw, Patrick, *Franklin D. Roosevelt.* New York: Pearson Longman, 2004.

Rosenman, Samuel I., *Working with Roosevelt.* New York: Harper & Brothers, 1952.

Roosevelt, Eleanor, *This I Remember.* New York: Harper & Brothers, 1949.

Roosevelt, Elliott, ed., *The Roosevelt Letters.* Three Volumes. London: George G. Harrap & Co., 1950.

Roosevelt, Elliott, and James Brough, *The Roosevelts of the White House: A Rendezvous with Destiny.* New York: G. P. Putnam's Sons, 1975.

Roosevelt, Franklin D., *Public Papers and Addresses of Franklin D. Roosevelt,* Samuel I. Rosenman, comp. New York: Random House, Macmillan, Harper and Bros., 1938–1950.

Salmond, John A., *The Civilian Conservation Corps, 1932–1942.* Durham, NC: Duke University Press, 1967.

Schieber, Sylvester J., and John B. Shoven, *The Real Deal: The History and Future of Social Security.* New Haven: Yale University Press, 1999.

Schlesinger, Arthur M., Jr., *The Crisis of the Old Order 1919–1933.* Boston: Houghton Mifflin, 1957.

Schlesinger, Arthur M., Jr., *The Coming of the New Deal.* Boston: Houghton Mifflin, 1959.

Schlesinger, Arthur M., Jr., *The Politics of Upheaval.* Boston: Houghton Mifflin, 1960.

Smith, Jean Edward, *FDR.* New York: Random House, 2007.

Tugwell, Rexford G., *The Democratic Roosevelt.* Garden City, NY: Doubleday & Co., 1957.

Tugwell, Rexford G., *FDR: Architect of an Era.* New York: The Macmillan Co., 1967.

Tugwell, Rexford G., *In Search of Roosevelt.* Cambridge: Harvard University Press, 1972.

Tull, Charles J., *Father Coughlin and the New Deal.* Syracuse: Syracuse University Press, 1965.

Warren, Donald, *Radio Priest.* New York: Free Press, 1996.

Williams, T. Harry, *Huey Long.* New York: Alfred A. Knopf, 1969.

Wood, Gordon S., *The Creation of the American Republic 1776–1787.* Chapel Hill: University of North Carolina Press, 1969.

Wood, Gordon S., *The Radicalism of the American Revolution.* New York: Alfred A. Knopf, 1992.

Index

About the Author

MARIO R. DINUNZIO is professor emeritus of history at Providence College in Rhode Island, where he has taught for many years and has served as director of the Development of Western Civilization Program. His other books include *Theodore Roosevelt, Theodore Roosevelt: An American Mind, Woodrow Wilson,* and *American Democracy and the Authoritarian Tradition of the West.*